NEGRO-JEWISH RELATIONS IN THE UNITED STATES

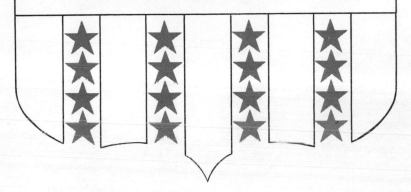

Negro-Jewish Relations in the United States

PAPERS AND PROCEEDINGS OF A CONFERENCE
CONVENED BY THE CONFERENCE ON
JEWISH SOCIAL STUDIES
NEW YORK CITY

THE CITADEL PRESS / NEW YORK / 1966

First published in *Jewish Social Studies*, 1841 Broadway, New York, N. Y. 10023 (January 1965), a quarterly journal devoted to contemporary and historical aspects of Jewish life. Edited by Salo W. Baron, Emeritus Professor of Jewish History, Literature, and Institutions at Columbia University, and Abraham G. Duker, Professor of History and Social Institutions and Director of Libraries, Yeshiva University, Editors; and Meir Ben-Horin, Professor of Education at The Dropsie College for Hebrew and Cognate Learning, Managing Editor.

CONTENTS

INTRODUCTION

The Conference on Negro-Jewish Relations, at which the papers published in this volume were first presented, reflects the conviction of leaders and scholars on both sides that a candid exploration of the complex of issues generated by these relations would contribute to the relaxation of rising tensions, and to a more effective coordination of efforts on behalf of joint and mutual concerns.

Such a conviction is well within the frame of reference of the sponsoring organization. For, since its founding over three decades ago, the Conference on Jewish Social Studies has sought to bring to bear both the temper and the conclusions of historical and sociological scholarship on pressing social problems which, one way or another, affect Jewish communities here and abroad.

It was the idea of the eminent philosopher, the later Professor Morris Raphael Cohen of the College of the City of New York, and Professor Salo Wittmayer Baron, now emeritus professor of Jewish history, literature and institutions at Columbia University, both founders of the Conference on Jewish Social Studies (originally Conference on Jewish Relations) that sound policies and intelligent action in Jewish affairs must be based on the most accurate and reliable information obtainable through scientific research. At a meeting presided over by Albert Einstein, they launched the Conference in 1933 as a non-partisan association of scholars and laymen united in the belief that those who must take action or solve problems need facts instead of guesses, conclusions reached through attention to conditions, methods and goals rather than theories reflecting wishful thinking or "committed" partisanship hardened beyond correction.

It is not surprising, therefore, that in 1964 the Conference on Jewish Social Studies devoted its annual meeting to what by then had become a pressing social problem affecting the American Jewish community. This pressure came at the same time from within and from without. Impelled by some of the deepest and most tenaciously defended insights of the Jewish people's old-new civilization, most spokesmen for American Jews found themselves vigorously supporting the Negro aspirations for equality in the United States. Many Jews became involved in the struggle and some suffered martyrdom at the hands of the foes of Negro emancipation. To some Jews, the cause of Negro freedom overshadowed any other concern, including the concern for continuity and advancement of Judaism as a religio-ethnic way of life, way of thought, and way of selfless devotion. Soon voices were raised challenging such all-out absorption. Tension began to rise between those who, in the name of Jewish and American loyalties, involved themselves in the civil rights struggle to the exclusion of all other interests and those who, also in the name of Jewish and American loyalties, cautioned against radicalism on its behalf as well as against unconditional self-immersion in its strategy and tactics.

From the Negro side came, indirectly or directly, calls for active participation. The presence of persons identified as Jews at important turning points —or pressure points—was usually warmly welcomed. At the same time, the charge was made either that the degree of participation fell short of expectations or that—to use terms of modern Jewish history—Negroes needed not so much emancipation as auto-emancipation. In some areas Jews, in fact, happened to occupy positions that appeared to block the Negro advance. To the more discerning Negroes, it was these blocking positions that mattered, while to the less fastidious, generalizations came easily from some Jews to most Jews. The option of virulent antisemitism as a tool of mass-direction, mass-consolidation, and mass-inflammation emerged for some of the socially less conscionable and individually more irritable among Negro leaders and followers.

Clearly, the time was ripe for a full-scale, frank, yet scholarly exchange of views. The result was the Conference on Negro-Jewish Relations in the United States, convened on Sunday, May 3rd, 1964, by the Conference on Jewish Social Studies in New York City. The papers and proceedings presented were first published in *Jewish Social Studies,* vol. xxvii, no. 1 (January 1965). They are now offered in book form in response to the wider interest engendered by the first presentation and in response to the need for further informed debate on an issue touching the nature and the direction of the republic.

MEIR BEN-HORIN

THE PARTICIPANTS

HORACE MANN BOND, dean, school of education, Atlanta University, is the author of *The Search for Talent, Education for Production, Education in Alabama, The Education of the Negro in the American Social Order*. From 1945-57 he served as president of Lincoln University. He is chairman of the board and former president of the African-American Institute of the American Society of African Culture.

HOWARD M. BROTZ teaches at Smith College, Northampton, Mass. He is the author of *The Black Jews of Harlem* (1964).

DAVID CAPLOVITZ, assistant professor of sociology, University of Chicago and a senior study director of the university's National Opinion Research Center, is the author of the Anti-Defamation League report *Swastika 1960: An Analysis of the Epidemic of Incidents In America* and of *The Poor Pay More*.

SIGMUND DIAMOND is professor of historical sociology at Columbia University and managing editor of the *Political Science Quarterly*. He is the author of *The Reputation of the American Businessman* (1955) and such other works as *A Casual View of America: The Home Letters of Salomon de Rothschild* (1961).

ABRAHAM G. DUKER, an editor of JEWISH SOCIAL STUDIES, is professor of history and social institutions and director of libraries, Yeshiva University.

BEN HALPERN, associate professor of Near Eastern and Judaic studies, Brandeis University, is the author of *The Idea of the Jewish State* and *The American Jew*.

CLEVELAND ROBINSON, a member of the New York City Commission on Human Rights, serves as treasurer of District 65, Retail, Wholesale and Department Stores Union, AFL-CIO, New York City, and national vice-president of the Negro American Labor Council. He was administrative chairman of the March on Washington, August 28, 1963.

BAYARD RUSTIN, an eminent Negro leader, has served as first secretary of the Congress of Racial Equality, as special assistant to Dr. Martin Luther King, and as a deputy director of the March on Washington, August 28, 1963.

1

MORRIS U. SCHAPPES, editor of *Jewish Currents,* is the author of *A Pictorial History of the Jews in the United States, 1654-1965,* and editor of *A Documentary History of the Jews in the United States, 1654-1875;* of *Selections from the Prose and Poetry of Emma Lazarus;* and of *The Letters of Emma Lazarus, 1868-1885.*

LEO SROLE is professor of sociology, Downstate Medical College, State University of New York. He is co-author of *Mental Health in the Metropolis* and *Social Systems of American Ethnic Groups.*

Other participants in the Conference were Harold U. Ribalow, author and editor, and Emanuel Muravchik, national director of the Jewish Labor Committee.

The Conference sessions were chaired by Professor Salo W. Baron, Professor Joseph L. Blau, and by Rabbi Mordecai Waxman.

NEGRO ATTITUDES TOWARD JEWS

By Horace Mann Bond

This paper as presented was intended to be a first draft of a more formal statement.

On reflection, however, I began to realize that, at best, I was involved in describing personal reactions that in fact I did not myself fully understand. I am not a psychiatrist; and I believe that expert knowledge of the human mind is a prerequisite to the understanding of the complex of attitudes and sentiments involved in racial attitudes. I, therefore, decided to let the manuscript stand for what it was: a highly personal document that makes no pretension to being an authoritative, or even informed, exposition of the "attitudes" to be found among a group now numbering some twenty million human beings.

I am extremely gratified to see listed as a discussant, Dr. Srole, a distinguished sociologist with much experience in research involving psychiatric problems. I rather think that he is better qualified to understand the subject, and what is revealed unwittingly in my paper, even better than I. I therefore present this paper, principally for what it is worth to Dr. Srole, and to other students of the depths of the human mind.

I

Let me preface this statement by telling you about something that happened to me in Atlanta, Georgia, in the Fall of 1916; I was then twelve years old.

My family had but shortly before moved to Atlanta from the small Alabama town of Talladega; I had lived there, as before in similar settings, in the sheltered environment of a small Negro missionary college founded and operated in the New England Puritan tradition; in which tradition, indeed, both of my parents had received their college education.

I was walking along a street near my house, and had to pass a small grocery store located in our neighborhood. There was a small boy—perhaps six years old—looking through the picket fence that surrounded the store. As I passed, he began to chant: "Nigger, Nigger, Nigger, Nigger." You may not believe it; but this was the first time I could remember anyone calling me a "Nigger." And my response still surprises me; I retorted to the boy,

3

"You Christ-killer!" And the little boy burst into tears, and I have felt badly about it ever since.

For one thing, it is quite impossible for me to understand how that "bad" word came into my vocabulary. I did immediately classify it with one of the "bad" words that I had been taught never, never, never, to use; and I certainly never heard it at home, unless from one of my older and more sophisticated brothers. I cannot recall any talk about Jews in my home, except, of course, about biblical Jews; and what with prayers before each meal, and scripture reading morning and night, and three church services on Sunday, and daily Chapel at school, one did hear a great deal about the People of Israel. The only foreigners about whom strong feelings were generated in my home, were the "terrible Turks," who were then supposed to be massacring the Armenians, and for whom our Church was raising money; and the Belgians, who were then (1916) suffering, we thought, their due reward in German brutality, for having cut off the hands of the Congolese when they failed to meet their rubber quotas! A Negro missionary who had been expelled from the Congo for exposing atrocities there was a family friend and frequent visitor in our home.

A long time later, still worrying about the little boy whom I had made cry because I called him a Christ-killer (after he called me a Nigger), I read the re-telling of the story of the Leo Frank lynching that took place August 17, 1915. It was alleged that young Frank, the Jewish manager of a textile factory, had raped and murdered one of his young white employees. Through his newspaper the demagogue, Tom Watson, filled the air with anti-Jewish venom; and Leo Frank was taken from a jail and hanged by a mob.

We moved to Atlanta one year after the lynching. I now think that, somehow, the word I used hung immanent in the Atlanta air; and, somehow, it had entered my mind, and remained there like a knife, waiting only for opportunity for release. But of course the thought that Christ had been killed, and by the Jews, and that this little boy was such a one, may have had a more ancient basis in my twelve-year old mind than I can now bring myself to admit.

II

I mention this forty-eight year old memory, because in it may lie the answer to the mystery and the implications of the question: "What are Negro attitudes toward Jews?" The boy was my first identified and catalogued Jew; he was the child of a Jewish family that kept the small grocery store in our neighborhood; and this pattern of first contact and association with the idea of "Jew" must be characteristic of the vast majority of American Negroes.

Or, in those days in Atlanta, the Jew was the man who kept the pawnshop on Peter, and Decatur, Streets, where I sold papers on a Saturday; he was the man who operated the clothing store where my father took his five boys occasionally to lay in a stock of clothes.

I now live in that same neighborhood in Atlanta. I think that the attitudes of my closest Negro acquaintances—most of them middle-class school teachers, physicians, social agency and business employees—toward Jews now find a focus in housing, perhaps the tenderest spot in the body of the Negro community in Atlanta. "Some Jews have bought up that urban re-development land and are putting up shoddy apartments they call 'Nigger housing' on it"; "The Jews have a stranglehold on the liquor stores in this town"; or, referring to our Jewish restaurateur, Gus Lebedin, who refuses to desegregate his place but explains: "I'm a Jew and I know what persecution means; but I'm not persecuting anybody. I just want the right to run my business as my customers want it run,"—and my friends say, "There's a Jew for you." A similar reaction was that of a friend who reacted somewhat unappreciatively to Senator Goldwater's statement, that "I am a half-Jew and I can sympathize with those who are discriminated against; but we ought to depend on the growh of the moral consciousness of the community and Nation, rather than on the extension of federal controls that will take away other people's rights." My friends said, "There's political genius for you; half-Jew, and all fascist. He'd kill more Negroes than Hitler killed Jews, to be elected President of the United States."

These random observations cannot, of course, be taken as representing the basic attitudes of the twenty million members of the Negro community toward Jews. I do believe that there are basic differences between attitudes of the white, "Gentile," community toward Jews, and those held by the generality of Negroes. These differences have their roots in the broad caste and class differences between the two communities.

In preparing this paper, I found it instructive to read Hugo Valentin's book on *Anti-Semitism*, published in 1935. He described it as "seen by" various groups—Jew and Gentile—and identified causes:

As Seen By—	The Cause Seemed To Lie In—
Orthodox Jews	Punishment for the sins of the Jews; an inevitable result of the dispersion, and the Godlessness of the Gentiles
Neo-Orthodox	Result of atavistic habits of thought "doomed to disappear"
Zionists	Result of existing national or cultural disparities between the Jews and the traditional anti-Jewish bias; racial antisemitism consciously or unconsciously defends itself against alien influences (Herzl); not only brutality, business jealousy, religious intolerance, but "presumed self-defeat"
Socialists	Marxists hold that antisemitism is the product of competitive jealousy, used by the powerful to exploit ancient prejudices and popular ignorance, diverting the fury of the impoverished classes from their real enemies.

Coudenhove-Kalergi .... (Freud)	Sense of inferiority; religious fanaticism; "Christ-killers."
Bernstein and Zweig .... (Added from Bettelheim and Janowitz, *Dynamics of Prejudice*)	Instinctive feeling of hostility; differences; the emotional disturbance of using antisemitism as a means of ridding one's consciousness of guilt. Hatred follows law of least resistance; a special case of the hatred of foreigners.
Others	Concern with status is more closely related to antisemitism than is authoritarianism, and the relationship between authoritarianism and anti-semitism may be largely explained by their mutual relationship to concern with status.

The differential class distribution of the Negro population must be appreciated before its attitudes toward Jews can be categorized. If this population be distributed according to Lloyd Warner's *Index of Status Characteristics,* or by any listing of occupations by social class, it becomes obvious that the Negro in America is either essentially the most degraded and inferior being in the land; or that he has been the victim of the most degrading system in the history of all human cultures. His life on this continent has been a succession of what one might call "deculturating" experiences. Up to 1865. the 90 percent of the Negro population that was slave, was not the object of a positive "culturative" influence; the "culture" applied to them was intended to produce more and better slaves. The 10 percent of the population that was free, prior to official emancipation, was in scarcely a better position. The efforts made since emancipation to bring this group into the mainstream of human culture as it exhibited itself in the U.S. have been extremely feeble. and in many instances, negative; neither religious nor political agencies have exercised much more than a passive overview of the progress the ex-slave was expected to make toward approximation to the dominant culture.

The American Negro, in this hit-or-miss endeavor, has gradually acquired certain traits of the culture—to a degree. The Negro acquired the language according to the extent that facility in its use was helpful to the master, in the process of exploiting the labor of the slave. Skills for use in various occupations were acquired on the same basis and for the same reasons. Standard forms of social organization—including the family—were acquired similarly.

The 10 per cent of the population that is Negro is represented in the professions and in technical and kindered occupations by 2.5 per cent of all Americans so employed. Even here a percentage this large is due to the employment of Negroes in occupations where they enjoy a "captive" market, due to segregation; school teaching is such an occupation. Negro males are 0.4 tenths of one percent of all engineers in the U.S.; they are 0.8 tenths of one percent of all architects; and, on the other end of the scale, this tenth of the nation that is Negro provides from 30-35 percent of the unemployed. They are even a higher proportion of what Lloyd Warner designates as his "lower-lower" social class.

Even more than did the European peasant and much more than the typical white American "Gentile," the Negro looks at the Jew across class lines slanted upward from lower class to middle class and upper middle-class status. If, indeed, concern for status in a competitive system is one of the chief roots of antisemitism, Negro attitudes must vary largely from those of his fellow, but white, American "Gentiles."

III

Attitudes toward Jews—either negative, or positive—have always been, and are now, part and parcel of the American culture. In the process of acculturation of sorts, the Negro has absorbed the cultural traits characteristic of the social and economic class to which he belongs—with variations, resulting from the unique caste status assigned to Negroes.

One aspect of the variations is that the existence of a common white oppressor frequently leads the Negro to consider the Jew as just another variety of white man who is out to take advantage of him and who seldom varies from the sentiments and attitudes and exploitative activities of all of the other white people he knows. It was characteristic that when Governor Wallace of Alabama was campaigning recently in Wisconsin, he felt it necessary to rebut charges of bigotry against "foreigners" leveled at him, by bringing up from his State a delegation of such persons to serve as exhibits of the popularity of his views among them. Calculated to appeal to the various national minorities in Wisconsin, the Governor's approving entourage included a Pole, a Greek, an Italian—and a Jew.

It is my considered view that Negro attitudes and actions toward Jews that are frequently interpreted as "antisemitic" actually lack the sinister thought-content they are sometimes advertised as holding. The occasional riots against small businessmen and landlords in Harlem—persons who may happen to be Jews—do not, in my opinion, actually possess the "classic" emotional load of aggression against a Jewish "race" or "religion," that has been considered the essence of "antisemitism." Our Southern newspapers like to display Northerners and Negroes as beings who are as prejudiced as they themselves are accused of being. Recently, when the Atlanta press reported the incident of an attack by a group of young Negroes on Jewish school children in New York, it was with a banner headline: "Negroes in Antisemitic Assault in New York." Although I make the judgment from 900 miles away, I think that such an assault would have taken place if the children and teachers involved had been Catholic or Italian or Swedish and placed in a situation accessible to attack; the children attacked were not so much Jewish, as they were white.

It is true that for the first time in American history we now have a well-organized group within the Negro community that is professedly anti-semitic. I refer to the Muslims who are called "Black" Muslims. Even here I believe that the expressed venom toward the Jew stems as much from the fact they are thought of as being among the white oppressors as being Jews. As part of my homework for this Conference I interviewed the minister of the Atlanta Temple (Mosque) (now transferred to Philadelphia), Jeremiah X. He was quite willing to be quoted, as he said the sentiments he expressed represented official policy:

> As a Muslim, the Jews are the Negro's worst enemies among whites. Unlike the other whites, Jews make it a practice to study Negroes; thus they are able to get next to him better than the other whites. He uses the knowledge thus obtained to get close to the Negro, thereby being in a position to stab him with a knife.
>
> We regard him as the real Devil of the Bible where it is said, "those who say they are Jews but are not, but are of the synagogue of Satan." Through their control of the press and of other mass media they are able to make the public feel sorry for Jews. It is so bad today that anybody who speaks out against Jews is immediately clobbered as "antisemitic."
>
> They have made the Negroes to believe that their sufferings have been greater than those of the Negro in America. They duped Sammy Davis into believing that the Jews' struggle was greater in America than that of the Negro (a statement he made when he adopted the Jewish faith).
>
> They infiltrate the Negro neighborhood with stores, and they exploit the Negro more than any other white group—housing, food, clothing—controlling the three basic things Negroes need. They claim to be friendly with Negroes but, when pushed to the wall, they are more injurious, more ruthless, than other whites.
>
> Their oppression of the Palestinian, Jordanian Arabs proves they can be just as ruthless as the Germans who, they claimed, tried to destroy them. The Jews are not a race, but a religion . . . In the Koran it is said, "Do not take Jews or Christians for friends; they are not your friends, but only to themselves . . . "
>
> Jesus himself said (John 8:44) the Jews were devils; we Muslims cannot have any more love for them than Jesus had.

The real basis of religious and racial attitudes, as I have tried to suggest, is obscure; as, indeed, the heart of man is obscure. I refer again to Valentin's book on antisemitism. As one re-reads this book and reflects on what happened in Europe after he published it, one sees that even a serious student of *Judenhass* did not have the slightest conception of the extent to which Hitler and the Germans were prepared to carry their hatred of Jews.

If the fate of the Jew in nazi Germany has taught us anything, it is that man has greater capability for wickedness than anyone has ever had a reason to suspect; even by 1935. The attitudes of Negroes toward Jews and the attitudes of Jews toward Negroes reveal a varied kaleidoscope of human capability for good but also for wickedness. My opinion is that we have not done more, in the study of attitudes and their sources—and their possible outcomes—than look through a glass, darkly. As a non-professional reporter on Negro attitudes, I must confess to little more than a superficial guess or combination of guesses. I really do not know.

If religion and emotions engendered by religious teachings are indeed a basic key, we need to note that the religion of the Negro slave early identified the group with the history of the Jewish people. Perhaps this feeling of identification is disappearing; but as a small child, I remember singing, not often in *our* church, because we used the Congregational Puritan hymnal, but at least in Sunday School, and always in school—even in a Congregational Church School—such songs as "Go Down, / Moses, way down, in Egypt land; / tell old Pharaoh, Let My People Go"; and, "Little David, Play on your harp, / Hallelu, Hallelu / Little David, play on your harp, Hallelu"; and "Joshua fit the battle of Jericho, Jericho, Jericho / Joshua fit the battle of Jericho / And the walls came a-tumbling down!"

I am not enough of a psychologist to assess the influence of such a tradition on the Negro mind, in the formation of attitudes toward Jews. Yet nearly forty years ago I had a position with the Julius Rosenwald Fund that required me to visit a great many of the schools erected with the help of that philanthropist in Southern rural areas.

I would defy anyone who said that there was any idea of antisemitism among the simple people I saw. The depth of gratitude felt by them for Mr. Rosenwald's assistance was enough to make one weep; especially as you realized that even this enormous philanthropy was only a drop in the bottomless bucket of needs that these people had in the brutalizing, dehumanizing, deculturative society in which they and their children—and their grandchildren, now living here in New York and Brooklyn—had to grow up. If anything, I felt that the edge of their gratitude was sharpened by the sense of Rosenwald's generosity coming as an appropriate gesture of help from an elder brother in the family of oppression. Their old familiar friend, the people of Israel who had once suffered in Egypt land, as they now were doing, had not forgotten them or forgotten the history of their own people.

And I have frequently reflected, also, that much of the sharpest feeling among Negroes about Jews arises from a feeling that this man has especially let you down; he, of all men, ought to know what it was like; and how it had been; but, as Jeremiah X told me, he turns out to be as bad, or even worse, than those other white devils.

THE NEGRO-JEWISH COMMUNITY AND THE
CONTEMPORARY RACE CRISIS

By Howard Brotz

The subject of my paper this morning is the Negro-Jewish community in New York. I shall first give a brief sociological analysis of the character of this sect, the impulse behind its aims, and the relationship between these and a broader stream of Negro thought and opinion. I shall then discuss what implications I believe that all this presents for an understanding of the Negro problem today.

As is perhaps well known to all of you, there has been for what is now over forty years a number of small sects of Negroes or so-called Negroes in Harlem who call themselves Black Jews or Ethiopian Hebrews. They abstain from pork, worship on Saturday, use Hebrew in their services, wear skull caps and prayer shawls. But at root what constitutes these sects is the belief that the so-called Negro race is misnamed, is not really a race but a nation which was robbed of its name, its religion and its culture by the slaveowner who then imposed upon the slaves an alien and false religion to weaken their morale, to make them feel that they owed everything to him for redeeming them from pagan superstitions. The Black Jews, on the contrary, believe that the so-called Negroes are really the lost tribes of the House of Israel. As such they believe that they have recovered their true identity and their true religion—the law—which makes them simultaneously independent of and superior to the whites who enslaved them. But why are they Ethiopian too, which seems to complicate things?

To solve this puzzle it may suffice to note that this sect is part of Ethiopianism, a broad movement in American Negro religion (and also in South and Central Africa). This movement, which goes back to the nineteenth century with certainty and perhaps even earlier was shaped by the interpretations which countless preachers placed on diverse biblical passages among which the crucial one perhaps is Ps. 68:31, "Ethiopia shall soon stretch out her hands unto God." By "Ethiopia" was meant not what we today mean by Ethiopia, *i.e.,* a particular country, but rather Africa as a whole. Ethiopian was synonymous with African or with the black people of Africa. The Negro's identification with the Ethiopian of the Bible thus became the basis of a nationalism, of a self-re-evaluating nationalism which has had in some cases militantly anti-white dimensions. In Nyasaland an uprising took place in 1915 under the leadership of a zealot named Chilembwe who, educated at an American Negro seminary, was animated by the principle of "Africa for the Africans," which was a deduction of Ethiopianism.

Taking the United States, the West Indies, and Southern Africa collectively for the moment, we may say, first, that the political goals of this movement have varied with the conditions at the time. Forty years ago, for example, Ethiopianism was feared in South Africa as an inflammatory force. Today these separatist churches are preoccupied with the economic advance of their members in a separatist framework and, not surprisingly, are prepared to seize the opportunities which are being created for this by the government's overall race policy. Second, the precise religious contents of the specific Ethiopic sects have varied. This is not surprising, in view of the tremendous freedom for innovation and fissure which the religious tradition broadly permitted. Only in the United States did Ethiopianism evolve into Ethiopian Judaism, although in superficial respects there are inclinations towards this in some sects in South Africa and the West Indies, such as in the use of symbols like the Star of David. Only in the United States, however, did this identification lead to a desire to approximate the forms of worship of rabbinic Judaism, as contrasted with what one may call the Judaistic idiosyncrasy which has been a feature of Anglo-Saxon Protestantism since the seventeenth century, such as, for example, in Seventh Day Adventism and in the Mormons. The reason for this, certainly in part was the presence of a large number of Jews with whom the Negroes came in contact, however superficial and transitory the contacts may have been. The association of Ethiopian and Hebrew had been made long before the first Ethiopian Hebrew ever laid eyes on a Jew. Yet the discovery that there were Jews, white or not, who practiced a complicated, dignified, esoteric, and what was without any doubt a non-Christian ritual, could not fail to affect their practices in many ways by providing an obvious model. This contact took place as the Negroes moved out of the rural areas of the South and the West Indies to the urban North. Ethiopianism, which took over the self-help emphasis of Booker T. Washington, also admired the Jewish people for their pride, their refusal to assimilate, their communal solidarity, and for their energy in lifting themselves up.

Now the Jewish world, for its part, has wondered what to make of these sects ever since it first discovered them; and there has naturally been a good deal of curiosity about them. While Judaism knows no racial barrier to conversion, Sammy Davis, Jr. being only the most celebrated of such examples, it is nonetheless true that the phenomenon of a Negro being a Jew cannot help but strike the Jew as being unusual. They naturally are led to wonder: Are these people really Jews? How did they get to be Jews in the first place? What practices do they observe? I will not now say anything further than what I have said above or more fully in my book about these questions or about the relationship which might evolve between the Jewish world and these sects. I merely note that in focusing one's observations about the sect on the question of their relationship to the Jewish world, one may lose sight of the sociologically more important question which the sect presents. And this is the effect on their behavior of their whole moral and socio-political outlook of which their religion is just a part.

What is the essence of this outlook? If we take our bearings initially by what is most important for these people, we see at once the theme of the Chosen People. Their belief that they are not a despised race but the descendants of the patriarchs gives them a pride and an inwardness which they never before possessed. They feel that they have recovered their own, that they now have a house of their own. As such they have on this level of belief a basis of self-sufficiency. Far from being ashamed of being black, they are proud of it. They are in Jewish terms non-assimilationists. This self-sufficiency or pride includes an active emphasis upon self-help and the introduction of a moral ordering of their family lives. From my sociological point of view it is this rather than the purely religious considerations which is the crucial aspect of this sect. To say, as is the case, that there is no crime or juvenile delinquency in this sect is the least that can be said about them. Much more important is the fact that they have formed a community and a private suburban housing development which enabled a number of the sectaries to leave the slums. Thus their vindication of the dignity of the black man has not simply remained on the plane of mere belief, but has led them to aspire to and achieve a significant measure of equalization as a community in behavior in the light of what they regard and what in fact are the standards of decent normal family life and social life prevalent in this country. By their own efforts they have achieved for themselves the basis of a rational self-esteem and the contentment which naturally flows from it. The Negro world, I think, may have something important to learn from the experience of this community.

Looking at the broad situation of the Negro in America today, one can hardly avoid noting that the protest movement which gained such momentum over the past year has run into an impasse. How we are to come out of this impasse will have a great deal to do with the future of this country. For from here on we—and that means of all races—will either take steps to solve the race problem in this country or we will let things drift until race relations could become so embittered that a solution becomes impossible. This would be a terrible blight on this country in which the race problem is really the only outstanding political problem.

In any sketch of this situation the obvious starting point is the fact that over the past years the Negro has achieved much, legally, politically, economically. Public stigmatization—by which I mean signs "White only," with which every Southern railroad station used to be plastered—has vastly diminished, together with Jim Crow. Signs still exist in places but one has to look for them. The best colleges are eager to accept qualified Negro applicants. The job ceiling has been raised. In fact, the stickiest problems with regard to discrimination are not at the top of the ceiling but at the lower middle ranks of the occupational structure. It is here, for example, that the Negro comes into competition with ethnic craft unions, who are in fact not so much anti-Negro as pro-themselves. In all, a sizeable Negro middle class has not only emerged but is expanding.

Yet with all this economic and social progress the Negro, collectively speaking, is more angry and frustrated than ever before, not to mention the amount of violence and disorder that has been a feature of race relations in the recent past. Sociologists see in this an exemplification of the general rule that people who are completely depressd aspire to nothing and in a mute way accept what they have. However, when they begin to acquire something, their aspirations are unlocked and stimulated, and they begin to measure their satisfaction not by what they have but by what they don't have. Granting that perfect equality cannot be achieved even in an intra-racial context, there will always be some inequality. This, linked rightly or wrongly to discrimination, is a basis for sustained discontent. Something of this sort is certainly a feature of the Negro protest as of other rising groups.

Beyond this generality there is something very specific agitating the Negro. This is his feeling that he is compelled by and large to live in a ghetto, by which he means not a gilded ghetto but rather a neighborhood which is inferior in every respect—physically, in its schools, communal services, and quality of life—to the prevalent standards of middle-class America. Faced with this fact of his condition, the Negro who wishes improvement for himself and his family seeks entry into white schools and neighborhoods. Of late we have heard schemes proposed to bring white and Negro children into each other's neighborhood schools. All this, of course, has been taken up by Negro protest organizations. In this they have been guided in their policy formulations by the 1954 decision of the Supreme Court which ruled that separated facilities were inherently unequal. While the ruling was aimed at legalized, categorical separation of the races, based on laws or ordinances that declared mixed schools to be illegal, the Negro leadership has attempted to extend this ruling to de facto segregation. This attempt has not had universal success. In fact, a woman in Boston won re-election to the school board on this very point.

I mention it because I believe that this is a legal quibble which conceals the real issue. (Recently the Supreme Court has refused to hear an appeal from a lower court which denied the relevance of the 1954 decision to all-Negro schools in Gary, Indiana, where the local school board had clearly not intended to superimpose a system of segregation on the city. This leaves the situation somewhat open. While school boards are not compelled to end the racial imbalance that is the by-product of residential concentration and to equate it with segregation, they are not prevented either from embarking on schemes for lessening it in the schools. I believe this relieves the situation from the strangle-hold of legal doctrinairism.) The real difficulty is the feeling, not of the Negro in general but of the Negro who believes that by virtue of his own social standards and way of life he is respectable and superior not only to disorganized Negroes but disorganized whites, and, at the same time, thinks he is too weak to pull up the standards of the Negro base in an all-Negro setting. Primarily for this reason he wants integration. He is sure that if whites are in a classroom, his own child will be taught better. In other words, he seeks integration not with whites *per se,* with whites just because they are whites. This would be integration to satisfy the legalism which is such an unfortunate element in the present situation. Rather, he seeks integration with whites of a certain social standard, whites who will help maintain those very social standards which he himself values, whites whom he regards as allies in the effort to maintain a valued way of life.

It is this type of reasoning, rather than legalist formulas, which is the respectable case for what is called positive integration. Any group of Negroes who would actively court the association of whites, who are so much inferior to them educationally, socially, morally, that their presence would pull them down; a group of Negroes who would seek such an association just because these others were white and just in order to satisfy what they think is the demand of the Supreme Court decision, would be preposterous. Such, in fact, is not the way Negroes or, for that manner, anyone else behaves.

There is pressure for positive integration, based very much on the considerations that it is the vehicle of improvement. This is very much intertwined with and distorted by legalism, but it is present in the desire. Now this desire has run into a rock of white resistance. Not, to be sure, everywhere. In the town in which I live there is integration. There are several Negro families out of 30,000 people. Among these are two Negro professors who are employed by Smith College. They obviously do not live in a Negro neighborhood, good or bad, because there aren't enough Negroes to compose one. This is not quite the situation in New York and Chicago. To understand the obstacles to integration in the big urban areas, with large concentrations of Negroes, one is inclined to cite first of all as a cause racial prejudice, by which I mean the unwillingness to have as a neighbor a person just because he is a Negro. This, of course, ranges through varying degrees of intensity, from some kind of phobia against any contact with Negroes to a disinclination to live in an all-Negro neighborhood. Here they may not feel at home, just as Jews did not feel at home in Italian neighborhoods.

But standing aside from race prejudice strong or weak is unfortunately, or, perhaps, fortunately, another factor, and this is the class differential between Negroes collectively and whites collectively. This is the real obstacle to integration. In fact, my view is that *the race problem is not really a race problem but rather a class problem, or perhaps a race-class problem.* Where the white doubts that if integration takes place he can still maintain the social standards he values, integration will be resisted. Where he has that confidence—for example, in a good private college—it can and will take place. The Negro who is qualified will in fact be invited in, will be wanted. His presence will be not simply the mere satisfaction of an abstract right or demand but rather the basis of what is really important in human relations, namely, friendship.

Where, however, the class differential between the two races arises as a factor, the whites will lack the confidence I spoke of, they will tend to bracket the Negro into the race-class category, and integration will be resisted. This is the impasse I spoke of initially. It happens where large numbers are involved. If the Negro tries to compel large-scale integration by legal means where the class differential is great, the white may take it as a threat to his way of life; he may be tempted to change the law. This is so because America, in a sociological sense, constitutes not so much a white society but a middle-class society. The ruling middle class will not tolerate proletarianization of its way of life; and the race problem, as I said before, is a problem fundamentally only in so far as it is connected with this fear.

Total or even large-scale integration or assimilation, which is the solution of the race problem, will not take place on an *individual* basis where sizeable groups of unequal class characteristics are brought together. The assimilation which will take place will be on a group basis, where the class and social inequality between the Negro as a collectivity and the whites will be radically lessened. This, in turn, will then permit assimilation on an individual basis to take place as a matter of course. In this manner, I believe, the Negro will and should be encouraged to follow the course of all the other minority groups in America's ethnically heterogeneous society who have sought to assimilate themselves and bring themselves up as groups to the prevalent norm.

The goal of the Negro people in this country then cannot possibly be described in such arid and abstract legal terms as desegregation or integration or positive integration. Their goal can be nothing less than transformation into a normal American ethnic community, with its pride and community loyalty which are based not on resentment or hatred of whites but on an inward self-respect resulting from achievement. This would be a community which has energy and in which the standards of the energetic are respected and set the tone. This, the social and economic elevation of the Negro people collectively in the United States, and nothing less than this, is *the* goal of the Negro. To the achievement of this goal all legal considerations are merely means.

The question arises why this goal, which is a social and economic project, has been identified with a legal question. The answer is that the Negro protest in this century was set in motion by a protest against legal segregation and discrimination. In their day, all the minority groups experienced discrimination of one sort or another. What was done to the Japanese during the war was in a way worse than what was inflicted upon the Negro, yet they very quickly made a tremendous come-back. But only the Negro was faced with institutionalized legal discrimination, a public reminder of a legally inferior status which faced him wherever he looked and which demoralized the Negro community. For the determined fight against this we are all beholden to the Negro leaders who did a service not only to themselves but to the whole country in removing this inequity from the supreme law of the land. But not all resultant effects were especially beneficial. Amidst the struggle *against* segregation, any emphasis upon self-help by means of thriving community institutions appeared to amount to acquiescsence in segregation. Appearances, however, can be deceiving. One need merely cite, in the first instance, the experience of the Jews, the Greeks, the Orientals, the Irish and every other ethnic group in this country. More significantly, one might cite the impressive record of the Negro himself who has been emancipating himself from as far back as the day when the first slave bought his freedom, to say nothing further of the work of the church, benevolent societies, Tuskegee, all of which arose out of the ranks of the Negro people themselves. And the Negro, for all the inequality and disparity between Negroes and whites collectively which still exist, has nonetheless made more progress in this country than any other race or ethnic group. *How ? + Why ?*

Curiously, the present phase of the struggle for civil rights has obscured this record of the Negro's own progress, and which he never ceased making even under the Jim Crow period. A doctrinairism has emerged which predicated the belief that the entire fate and career of Negroes is determined by whites, discriminating or non-discriminating, but which belies the progress which the Negro continued to make even under discrimination. This doctrinairism underlies an extremism present in the current struggle. It is shared both by whites and Negroes—and formulates the Negro's goals wholly in terms of demands upon whites. With the passage of the Civil Rights Bill it is perfectly possible that the situation will right itself. However, one ought to be mindful of the possibility of what is called the "white backlash" to point out its danger. By this I mean not only the counter-attacks, including violence of white segregationists who wish to keep the Negro depressed, but also the resistance of those whites, particularly in the North, to integration schemes that are projected without regard to such factors as number or social characteristics, where there is a reasonable fear that mass integration will result in a lowering of standards. A bifurcation of politics on the race issue that would cause these two groups to coalesce would be a disaster, and herein lies the danger of immoderate and doctrinaire integration schemes that lead whites to view them not as pulling the Negro up but rather as pushing the white down. While I do not believe this coalition will emerge and while I do not think it even necessary to dwell unduly on the possibility of it, enough has happened already to induce thoughtful whites and thoughtful

Negroes to consider what they can do to break through this cycle of reaction and counter-reaction.

The primary question is what can be done to fortify that Negro leadership which is concerned with both legal rights and the reconstruction of the Negro community.

Much more important than sermons or exhortations to the Negro, which can be properly regarded as offensive, is the simple but crucial recognition by whites of the Negro virtue which exists and which has always existed. I mean, of course, those Negroes who are concerned not only about freedom in a formal legal sense but with the preparation of their race for the proper use of freedom, with education, with family stability, in a word, with standards. These are the natural leaders of the Negroes as Americans. The task, now as always, is to support them, not so much with regard to their demands as their needs. The recently announced collaborative project between the Urban League and the American Jewish Congress for the stimulation of Negro business enterprises deserves high praise. This contributes to what I have described in my study as that open alliance between the Negroes and whites who stand for excellence and for the interdependent progress of both races. It is they who hold the key to the solution of the race problem.

Sects such as the Ethiopian Hebrews are of interest because of the fact that they have stood for the self-help impulse in Negro life. They are also of interest because of the mythology which they have constructed in order to assert this impulse with self-respect. In constructing such an anti-white mythology, they obviously put themselves out of range of being called "Uncle Toms." This is much more visible with regard to the Black Muslims. Because of the irrationality in their beliefs and also the hatred which is present in their outlook, they are no model for an American Negro leadership. But the self-help aspect can indeed be looked upon in its own light as valuable. The problem as I see it in the future is to detach this from the irrational context and make it part of the rational struggle for civil rights.

ON NEGRO-JEWISH RELATIONS—
A CONTRIBUTION TO A DISCUSSION

By Abraham G. Duker

There has been a good deal of interest in the subject,[1] but little solid research has been done on it. Not by accident, most writings by Jews (less so in Yiddish and Hebrew) resemble the ethical admonition (*mussar*) literature, urging repentance for alleged shortcomings in the treatment of the Negroes and more than full involvement in the struggle for equality.[2] Most writings by professionals employed by Jewish organizations are tinged with what I call the community relations complex.[3] One may question whether this *mussar* literature can be accepted as the true Jewish *vox populi*.

It is most difficult to evaluate without specific studies the varying attitudes of American Jews to the Negro problem. The limited communication between the Jewish leadership and public is another obstacle. American Jewry, numbering from 5,000,000 to 6,000,000 individuals, of different religious, cultural and geographical background, cannot be expected to follow a single pattern of behavior or thinking.

Jewish Efforts on Behalf of Negroes

The history of Jewish efforts on behalf of Negro welfare, which I hope will be written some day by competent historians, should not only include in its roster the names of Julius Rosenwald, of social workers, rabbis, lay leaders, of Jewish youths who have risked their lives in the South, but also of unassuming persons who have pioneered in race relations without

[1] The most useful bibliography is The American Jewish Committee, Blaustein Library, *Negro-Jewish Relations; A Selective Bibliography* (New York, April 30, 1963; mimeog.). The mimeographed bulletin by the same publisher, *Articles of Interest in Current Periodicals* brings the listing of magazine publications up to date. Of interest is also The American Jewish Committee, New York Chapter, Kleinfeld, M. J. and Levinson, Louise, eds., *Negro Press Digest* (mimeog.). The compilation of a full bibliography on the subject would be most desirable.

[2] For examples of this type of inward directed literature *see* Lurie, Walter A., *The Best Lack All Conviction. Some Reflections on the Role of Jewish Communal Agencies in the Crisis of our Times,* Association of Jewish Agency Executives of Philadelphia (Philadelphia, Dec. 5, 1963) (processed), 7 pp.; Vorspan, Albert, "The Negro Victory and the Jewish Failure," *American Judaism,* vol. xiii, no. 1 (1963), pp. 7, 50-52, 54.

[Of later vintage of this very popular literature are items ranging from admonitions by a professional, Vorspan, Albert, "Ten Ways Out for Tired Liberals," *American Judaism,* vol. xiv, no. 1 (1964) pp. 14-15, 57-58, to a warning by a Yeshiva College student, Prystowsky, Steven, "Negro Animosity Towards Jews Has Many Roots," *The Commentator* (*Yeshiva University*), vol. lix, no. 4 (March 25, 1964) p. 16.]

[3] What I term the "community relations complex," which causes those afflicted by it to view all human phenomena from their possible effects on the community relations of the Jews as a minority has by this time become if not a substitute for religion, at least a most important ingredient of it. *Cf.* my *Jewish Community Relations. An Analysis of the MacIver Report* (New York 1952). Examples of such thinking will be found in most publications of Jewish groups involved even partly or peripherally in community relations. A good example is Lipman, Eugene J. and Vorspan, Albert, *A Tale of Ten Cities: The Triple Ghetto in American Religious Life* (New York 1962).

18

fanfare or publicity.[4] This may help to balance the record of Jews in the South where they constitute a particularly vulnerable minority.

Obvious is a very wide participation of Jews in pro-integration activities, named the "Negro revolution," but more properly identified as the struggle for the completion of Negro emancipation. I venture to state that at CORE and SNCC meetings in larger cities and on the campus, on picket lines and at mass demonstrations, in publications, in audiences of forums, in short, as dedicated individuals, the number of Jewish participants is far beyond their proportion in the white population.

Community relations organizations, the B'nai B'rith Anti-Defamation League, the American Jewish Committee, the American Jewish Congress, the Jewish Labor Committee, the National Community Relations Advisory Council, local agencies have been very much involved, first in the legal aspects of the struggle for equality and later in the integration drive. Many, possibly even most, national organizations concerned with domestic affairs, are committed to it. In fact, I am tempted to speculate what might have happened in the 1930's and the 1940's if some of these defense bodies had been involved to the same degree in efforts to rescue Jews from Hitler genocide.

Jewish welfare institutions have for a long time not only maintained an open door policy to patients of all races but have been increasingly hospitable to them. As a general rule, Jewish hospitals have not followed the movement of the Jewish population, but have continued to expand in the former Jewish neighborhoods, with the consequence that Negroes and members of other "minorities" constitute the overwhelming majority of clinic patients and are well represented as bed patients. (Good examples are Mt. Sinai in New York and Michael Reese and Mt. Sinai in Chicago.) Jewish settlement houses and many community centers have been extending their open door policy and have been spearheading pro-integration activities in the local communities and on the national level. Interracial child adoption was initiated by a Jewish agency in New York. Child welfare agencies and their summer camps have been open to non-Jews and, I would say, particularly to Negroes. Many Federation welfare agencies have been emphasizing their services to the entire public rather than care of Jewish needs as the major rationale for their existence.[5] *so Lutherans + what*

---

[4] A good example is the role of Dr. Irving L. Greenberg in Atlanta, Ga., in pro-integration work right after World War II.

[5] On social services, *cf.* Glazer, Nathan, "Effects of Emerging Urban-Suburban and Anti Segregation Developments on Jewish Communal Service," *Journal of Jewish Communal Service*, vol. xli, no. 1 (Fall 1964) pp. 60-66 and Miller, Charles, "The Impact of the Integration Struggle upon Jewish Services," *ibid.*, pp. 67-74; my article, "The Problems of Coordination and Unity," in Janowsky, Oscar I., ed., *The American Jew, A Reappraisal* (Philadelphia 1964), pp. 331-32, 448 n. 15.

For an example of local community council activities, *see* Greenfield, Robert K., *Race Relations 1963: Implications for the Jewish Community of Greater Philadelphia. Report to the Board of Directors of the Federation of Jewish Agencies, July 1, 1963*, Jewish Community Relations Council of Greater Philadelphia (processed), 4 pp.; Jewish Community Relations Council of Greater Philadelphia, *A Program of Action for the Jewish Community in the Present Race Relations Emergency Adopted by the JCRC Board of Directors Wednesday, June 26, 1963* (processed), 7 pp.

Behind the Liberal Pattern

It is important that we understand the causes of this intensive interest in the Negro struggle on the part of so many Jews. This liberal pattern, so far in advance of that of the majority of the Christian white population, has been manifested also in political elections and has led to an intensive preoccupation with community relations. It stems from the Jewish tradition of social justice (usually called "prophetic" tradition), American democratic concepts, the classical Jewish minority position (though not always acknowledged) and the organizational structure of the Jewish community. Moreover, the impact of the nazi holocaust that has cost the lives of six million Jews has heightened the sensitivity of Jews to inequality and minority positions.

Not to be disregarded is the residue of radical sentiment, leftovers from the fellow-traveller fashion of the 1930's and 1940's when under the threat of nazism and the delusion of a Soviet society free from antisemitism, communism appeared to many as the only answer to Jew-hatred. However, Stalin's antisemitic maneuverings, especially the Doctors' Plot, Khrushchev's exposure of his predecessor, and continued Soviet antisemitism have drastically reduced the leftist ranks. The remnant has found a way of regaining its respectability and opportunities for penetration and recruiting through the Negro integration struggle. Trotzkyite and Maoite varieties are also active. Their influence in radicalizing the pro-integration movement and tactics will be increasingly felt by both the Negro and Jewish communities.

Special Demands on Jews

It is unfortunate that at the present stage there has been little frank dialogue between Jews and Negroes. In consequence of disappointments with the pace of integration, it would seem to me that more and greater demands are being made by Negro leadership on the Jewish community than on the Christian denominations which surely should be closer to the Negroes because of their adherence to the same religious faith. Such demands on Jews are sometimes veiled with threats. These are remindful of prolegomena to quotas, robberies, confiscations and pogroms. Demands for "Negroization" of Harlem stores are viewed by some Jews as too simliar to "Aryanization" propaganda in Germany. Because of bitter historical experience, Jews abhor the idea of quotas. They are uneasy about pressures for racial quotas, and not only as citizens are they concerned with attempts to abolish the merit system in the civil services. While some complaints about attitudes of some Jewish teachers or social workers to Negroes may be justified, most may well be due to the pressure for "Negroizing" the teaching and administrative staffs in Negro districts. Many Jewish school principals, teachers and social workers have shown extraordinary devotion to the Negro pupils and clients. Their achievements have not received due recognition.

Ignoring Jewish Contributions

Such fears and doubts are not eased by what appears to be the increasing tendency on the part of Negro spokesmen not to give recognition to pro-Negro activities by Jews, particularly Jewish organizations. For instance, Louis E. Lomax in his *The Negro Revolt* (New York: Signet Edition, 1963) omits the mention of the American Jewish Congress and American Jewish Committee, despite their long involvement in the struggle for equality, long before the momentous decision of the Supreme Court in 1954.[6] It is not a matter of gratitude, but of a balanced record and a basis for mutual understanding.[7] True, the struggle against antisemitism has proven that apologetics about Jewish contributions and patriotism have had little if any effect on rabid antisemites. Nevertheless, unless we can agree that the more decent elements can be influenced by pointing out such facts, we might just as well give up any educational approach to the cure of racism and antisemitism. Negro intellectuals could contribute more to this understanding. *Lousy after his approach*

On Collective Responsibility

No doubt, some complaints against Jewish storekeepers and landlords are justified. But the role of the Jewish retailer as a helper and adviser to the less sophisticated Negroes is being ignored, as are the special interests

[6] In his *When the Word Is Given. A Report on Elijah Muhamad, Malcolm X and the Black Muslim World* (New York 1964) (Signet Edition), Mr. Lomax treats attempts to rescind the deicide accusation against the Jews with contempt and disposes of the Jewish "chosen people" doctrine by citing an excitable student at a meeting at Columbia University Student Organization (pp. 64-66) in an unfair manner.

[7] The list of books ignoring the role of the Jews is too long to cite, nor have I perused the entire literature. To balance the picture, following is a list of works where the problem is treated more objectively or is given recognition: Frazier, E. Franklin, *The Negro in the United States* (revised ed.) (New York 1957), where the Julius Rosenwald Fund is mentioned. John Hope Franklin in his *From Slavery to Freedom. A History of the American Negroes* (2nd ed.) (New York 1956) refers to the Anti-Defamation League and the National Jewish Welfare Board, but omits the American Jewish Committee and American Jewish Congress. H. Harry Giles in *The Integrated Classroom* (New York 1959) accentuates the functions of "self-protection bodies" by "disadvantaged or minority groups," listing the three mentioned community relations agencies and the National Community Relations Advisory Council. He also credits them with "increased educational effort to deal with discrimination and social relationship by mass distribution of pamphlets . . ." (p. 129). Robert C. Weaver in *The Negro Ghetto* (New York 1948) singles out Philip Klutznick (pp. 162, 177). The dynamic role of Jews in urban centers with "well staffed organizations with a commitment to school equality and intergroup goals" is brought out by James Q. Wilson in his *Negro Politics* (Glencoe 1960), where the three leading community relations agencies are singled out in connection with the establishment of the New York State Commission on Discrimination in Housing, (pp. 151-2).

of Negro businessmen who have not given up the profit motive. There is also the factor of Negroes who work in Jewish establishments that has not been studied at all. This presents areas of both conflict and friendship. Jewish organizations and individuals have indeed pioneered in employing Negro white collar workers. Whatever the case, just as Negro leaders should not bear the blame for the behavior of all the Negroes, so the Jewish community cannot be held responsible for the actions of individual Jews, many of whom are not affiliated with any Jewish organizations and over whom the latter have no control. Just as responsible Negro leadership has the duty to give guidance to its community, to resist machinations of racist rabble rousers, lawless elements, Nasserite and communist agitators, similarly Jewish leadership should guide the Jewish community to do its duty and support Negro equality, taking into consideration Jewish communal needs and capacity, in the light of the dual role of the Jew as a member both of the larger community and of the Jewish group.

Priorities in Communal Allocations

In many cases Jewish communal involvement in integration has direct bearing on Jewish cultural and religious life. Priority in local allocations of Federations and Welfare Funds is generally given to such institutions, often at the expense of the chief Jewish survival needs, education and culture. In a pluralistic society and despite the expansion of the welfare state, large city federations have been continuing to carry out the functions of the government and general community agencies in their attempts to serve all at the cost of neglecting needs of Jewish clients and of Jewish survival.

The struggle for integration has strengthened this tendency. Jewish survivalist needs have not always received priority in the policies and activities of the community relations agencies. For instance, the danger in the reduction of available time for afternoon Jewish education due to school busing has been ignored by such agencies[8] in proposals for school integration. After the genocidal debacle of World War II, in the face of the massive campaign of cultural genocide against the Jews in the U.S.S.R. and of a global Nasserite plot to liquidate Israel, we, the remnants, are struggling for cultural and religious survival, and as a group we have rights to both. Some Negro spokesmen have shown little understanding of this aspect of Jewish life.

Causes of Negro Antisemitism

A good deal of this misunderstanding stems from the *sancta* and *mores* of the general society. For instance, Dr. Bond has made a blanket denial

---

[8] *Cf.* American Jewish Congress, Metropolitan Council, *A Program for Integrating New York City's Schools* (New York 1964) (processed).

that antisemitism had been a factor in the attack of youthful Negro hood-lums on the Lubavitch Yeshiva (Day School) pupils in the Bedford Stuyvesant section of Brooklyn in April 1964. I disagree with his view. His own cited childhood "Christ killer" reaction and the memoirs of a leading Negro writer[9] testify to the contrary. We should take it for granted that antisemitism among Negroes basically stems from the same sources which have nurtured Jew-hatred among white Christians, namely, theological deicide notions. These were translated into folklore, folkways and stereo-types and have led to pogroms, robbery, exiles, and murder. Negro Christians have been raised on the New Testament perhaps more than white Christians. It is likely that many have absorbed anti-Jewish theological teachings and folklore. In consequence of the genocide of the 6,000,000 Jews during World War II and in the face of Christendom's sorry record of rescue ef-forts, sensitive Christians have become aware of the disastrous role of the *odium theologicum* in spreading antisemitism. The Vatican, too, has begun to revise this nineteen-centuries-old psychological preparation for massacres. It will take a long time to change attitudes of individual Christians. The realization of this terrible wrong should eventually help to weaken the re-ligious basis of Jew-hatred among Negroes. Unfortunately, Islamic or Black Muslim anti-Jewishness may replace its Christian counterpart in some quarters. An honest dialogue cannot dismiss these aspects.

There are, of course, also other factors. The traditional position of the Jews as a scapegoat for all ills serves as a ready escape for Negroes who resent their own position on the lowest rung in American society. Actual and probably more so potential economical rivalry is felt among the rising Negro middle class, its professionals, business people and civil servants.[10]

---

[9] Thus, Richard Wright writes that "to hold an attitude of antagonism or distrust toward Jews was bred in us from childhood; it was not merely racial prejudice, it was part of our cultural heritage." *Black Boy* (New York 1945) p. 54. Cited from Wittenberg, Rudolph M., *Discipline in the Teens* (New York 1963), p. 24.

[10] This is not a new manifestation and we shall have to live with it for a long time to come. *Cf.* Myrdal, Gunnar (with the assistance of Richard Sterner and Arnold Rose), *An Ameri-can Dilemma. The Negro Problem and Modern Democracy* (New York 1944), p. 1190, n. 23. *Cf.* also St. Claire Drake and Horace M. Kayton in *Black Metropolis* (New York 1945) who cite antisemitic action against Jewish merchants as early as 1938, as well as other in-stances (pp. 197, 213, 432n, 249, 43n, 435-56 *passim*, 635).—The riots during World War II have produced a sizeable literature. In addition to those listed in the American Jewish Committee bibliography (*cf.* note 1), the following will be found useful: Wolf, Eleanor Paperno; Loving, Alvin D.; Marsh, Donald C., *Negro-Jewish Relationships* (Detroit 1944); Wedlock, Lunabelle, *The Reaction of Negro Publications and Organizations to German Anti-Semitism, Howard University Studies in Social Sciences,* vol. iii, no. 2 (Washington 1942); Stemons, James Sam, *As Victim to Victim. An American Negro Laments with Jews* (New York 1941); Zuckerman, Nathan, *The Wine of Violence, An Anthology on Anti-Semit-ism* (New York 1947), pp. 313-42, contains many items. *The Journal of Negro History* devoted a special issue, vol. x, no. 3 (July 1941) to "Racial Minorities and the Present In-ternational Crisis," which included several articles dealing with the Jewish problem.—For the immediate post-war era, *cf.* Laufer, Leo, "Anti-Semitism Among Negroes," *The Reconstruc-tionist* (Oct. 1948), pp. 10-17.

The Attack on the Lubavitch Yeshiva Students

I therefore disagree with Dean Bond's view that the attack on the pupils of the Lubavitch Yeshiva was directed against them only as whites and not as Jews. There is ample evidence that these children had been frequently insulted, attacked and intimidated as Jews long before the major outburst.[11] Many Jews cannot accept as valid the sociological apologetics by Negro leaders for attacks against a most pacific group that wants to be left alone, is unwilling to "run away" from its spiritual leaders and communal geographical center, and has no objections to integrated neighborhoods as long as they are safe.[12] Regardless of psycho-sociological motivations or apologetics, lawlessness in the large Northern cities presents a most important problem in Negro-white and in Negro-Jewish relations. I believe that desegregation cannot be attained without residential integration. In turn, this rests on the safety of individuals in and near mixed neighborhoods in the large cities. We may have to face resegregation of neighborhoods because of the flight of the white population and of the Negro middle classes before desegregation will have been appreciably advanced.

Research Needs

A conference of this type should at the very least raise the question of joint research projects on minorities, possibly on a world-wide scale. Studies of experience of Jews, Negroes and other minorities would be of more than academic value. The project of a history of the role of Jews in pro-Negro movements would not be complete without studying the adverse sides, Jews in anti-Negro movements as well as Negro pro-Jewish and antisemitic movements. Other projects are a comparative study of characteristics of Jews as a religio-cultural-national minority and of Negroes as a racial cultural minority. Surely, we can profit from comparative studies in immigrant adjustment and self-help, as both Negroes and Jews (outside the South) began as immigrants in the large cities. There is room for perceptive research on comparative reaction to persecution between Jews and Negroes, on protest movements, their failures and successes in different

---

11 Cf. "Yeshiva Youths Bitter After Attack by Negroes," *National Jewish Post and Opinion* (Indianapolis, May 1, 1964).—The only sizeable article on the Lubavitcher stimulated neighborhood self-defense is "The Maccabees Ride Again," *The Saturday Evening Post* (June 27-July 4, 1964), pp. 32-36. There was no rush of social scientists to study this effective instrument for residential integration.

In May-June 1963, a rabbinical writer complained that "in New York, where the Negroes have the most freedom, some behave toward Jews without much love, especially, many of their youths in mixed sections do not desist from annoying Jewish children with all hatred according to the well-known [antisemitic] custom and yeshiva directors can report on the sad details." Berger, J. S., "In the World of Judaism," *Hamaor* (Brooklyn) vol. xiv, no. 1 (Iyyar-Siwan 1963), pp. 31-33.

12 On the question of halakhic permission for Jews to live in endangered sections, *see* Reis, Sheneour Zisha, "On the Doubt Whether the Desecration of the Sabbath is Permitted because of the Risk of Life. An Examination of the Causes of Casualties in our Days," *Hamaor* vol. xv, no. 6 (Tammuz 1964), pp. 3-4.

societies. More light is needed on problems of group belongingness and identity. Dr. Bond referred to the Negroes' deculturation from African cultures and acculturation into American culture. Jews have been facing a similar situation since the beginnings of emancipation.

Underprivileged Groups

The acculturation of Jews into the secularized Christian-directed and centered culture (you may wish to call it Christian white culture) because of their uneven integration in the western and Jewish cultures has been responsible for the popularization of a negative Jewish self-image, colored by hostile non-Jewish views of the Jew. This process very often parallels that of the acculturation of the Negro child in the white culture. Negroes are an educationally underprivileged group in American life. However, Jews, too, are culturally and religiously underprivileged. Just as the Negroes constitute a minority in white society, Jews are a minority in Christian society and culture. An imaginative minority-survivalist approach to pluralistic society and culture in America is recommended as another research project. This requires a close study of pluralism in American life.

The Melting Pot vs. The Melting Pots

Does the American melting pot exist? Certainly one can agree that there is a common core of American culture, expressed in language, food, customs, attitudes and culture patterns in an era of restricted immigration and increasing impact of mass media and therefore increased uniformity, in other words, a general American melting pot. However, Americans continue to live in a number of sub-cultures or, as some would say, constituent cultures: religious, ethnic-religious, and racial. The most important medium for the expression or transmission of these sub-cultures are the sub-communities, constituting small melting pots, basically along racial and religious lines, the white Protestant, the white Catholic, the Negro (mainly Protestant), the Latin American, the Eastern Orthodox and along ethnic-religious-cultural lines, as in the case of the Jews. There are also smaller sub-communities and sub-cultures, such as the Indians and the Kalmucks. It may be safely assumed that the major racial-religious melting pots are here to stay for a long time to come.[13]

[13] For my theory of multiple melting pots along racial-religious lines, *cf.* my *Workshop in Jewish Community Affairs. Course 1. The American Jewish Community: Its History and Development. Syllabus for Session 1. The Jew in American Group Life* (New York, the American Jewish Congress, 1952) pp. 15-17 (mimeographed); in the discussion at the Tercentenary Conference on American Jewish Sociology in JEWISH SOCIAL STUDIES, vol. xviii (1955), p. 185; and in my "Jewish Attitudes to Child Adoption," in Schapiro, Michael, Ed., *A Study of Adoption Practice. Selected Scientific Papers Presented at the National Conference on Adoption January 1955*, vol. ii (New York, Child Welfare League of America, 1956), pp. 146-48. The theme has since then been taken up by other writers.

On Negro Jews

Dr. Brotz brought out the fact that the Negro Jews constitute separate enclaves. They are not a part of the mainstream of Judaism, either by origin or by Halakha (rabbinic law). Nevertheless, I have been assured that there is no discrimination against Negro Jewish children who attend Jewish day schools and afternoon schools. When Harlem still had white Jewish congregations, Negro Jewish children belonged to the Institutional Synagogue's Boy Scout troop, without any problems of race. It is likely that there will be more Negro Jews in the future through conversion and through mixed marriages of Jewish women and Negroes, whose offspring are Jewish, according to Jewish law. The Jewish community will have to be more sensitive to the needs of Negro Jews. This is our Jewish prime responsibility in integration.[14]

Pluralism, Assimilation and Survivalism

There is ambivalence and tension in the reaction of the members of the various melting pots to their double roles in the general, culture, community or melting pot and in the small melting pots. Parallels and contrasts between Jews and Negroes are of more than academic interest.

American Negroes are divided into several types of assimilationists who favor physical disappearance in the future racially integrated American "melting pot," either gradually through intermarriage or quickly through a social revolution, and survivalists who prefer to remain Negroes. The latter may be divided into integrationist-pluralists who visualize some kind of continued racial-cultural Negro group existence, and the self-segregationists or separatists, who favor self-sufficient "nationalist" or religious enclaves (Black Muslims), separate statehood or even emigration. The difficulties of a rapid physical assimilation of the Negro, barring a far-reaching leftist totalitarian social order, are obvious. It would seem that escapism among Negroes has been on the decrease.

Differences between survivalists and assimilationists have existed among Jews since emancipation's beginnings. In the United States they are reflected in ideologies, but perhaps more so in behavioral patterns and institutional policies.

Jewish survivalists are pluralists who question the desirability of the melting pot and therefore of the assimilation of the Jew. The gas chambers and crematoria have proved at least to one generation the bankruptcy of

14 On Negro Jews cf. also Fauset, Arthur Huff, "Black Gods of the Metropolis," Publications of Philadelphia Anthropological Society, vol. iii (Philadelphia 1944), chap. 7; Ottley, Roy, New World A-Coming (Boston 1943); Zuckerman, Edith and Botwinick, Irwin, "Negro Jewish Sect of Brownsville, Brooklyn, N. Y.," an unpublished term paper in my class at New York University in the Fall of 1950. The number of newspaper items and magazine articles is too numerous to be mentioned.—Tsaad Rishon (The First Step), an organization for integrating the Negro Jews into the Jewish community, was established in 1964.

assimilation in Europe. Nevertheless, the pressures of acculturation, Jewish deculturation and thereby de-Judaization have been increasing, with hedonism and deracination as their most visible hallmarks. Departure from the community through intermarriage and indifference follows. On the left it is assumed that assimilation cannot be attained under capitalism. Some will admit that it is not easy to attain it in the U.S.S.R. However, others are convinced that the Trotzkyite or Chinese-style Marxist utopia will realize what the "schismatic" Khrushchevian paradise of the present had not been able to achieve.

Integration Struggle and Escapism

In the United States escapism from Jewishness has also found expression in the integrationist movement. I know of cases of escapist identification of Jews with the integration struggle to the extent of extreme *jüdischer Selbsthass* and active antisemitism not unlike the types brought out in Theodore Lessing's classical study.[15] (Interestingly, at least one study of Negro-white intermarriage reveals that the majority of the white partners are Jews.)[16]

Minorities and the Western World

Minorities owe it to themselves to take a long-range view of their position. While sociology is important, history cannot be ignored in such assessment efforts. Jews have had to view their relationship to the environing societies from the vantage of centuries. It is unfortunate that not too many of them are sufficiently knowledgeable to take this long range view. In contrast, the experience of Negroes as a disadvantaged minority among whites is relatively a short one, not much over 300 years, painful though it has been. Negro ambivalence about the values of the "white" civilization is to be expected as are similar attitudes by Jews towards "Christian" civilization. Nevertheless, most Jews, whether in the Diaspora or in Israel, are not likely to divorce themselves from western civilization, because of its seeming or actual "built-in" antisemitic ingredients. Knowledgeable Jews know of Jewry's long symbiosis with western culture, its negative as well as positive aspects. They do not expect any better prospects for dignified survival and self-expression in other civilizations. A long-range view should lead to a similar view among Negroes.

The strident calls by some Negro intellectuals and propagandists that the Negro masses abandon the ship of American society or western civiliza-

[15] *Der jüdische Selbsthass* (Berlin 1930). Negro parallels, now on the decrease, are interesting.—Myrdal called attention to William H. Thomas's "vitriolic but well-written book, *The American Negro* (1901) that has, indeed, its best counterparts in some of the extreme expressions of antisemitism which, as is well known, are to be found in occasional writings by Jews" (*op. cit.*, p. 1190).

[16] *Cf.* Powledge, Fred, "Negro-White Marriages on Rise Here," *The New York Times* (October 18, 1963).

tion because there is nothing worthwhile left to rescue or to integrate in this system sound very militant. They may, however, contribute to a mass tragedy, with the Negroes potentially as the major victims.

On Leadership and Social Stability

The leadership of a minority has a responsibility both to its followers and to the total community. It is not incumbent upon a persecuted minority to supply its enemies with additional ammunition and thus to strengthen anti-minority feelings when, in the final analysis, its future depends on the majority's good will. It is not always possible to secure such friendship. In this respect American Negroes are in a much more fortunate position than European Jews had been in the recent past. Modern Jewish history has ample examples to offer of lack of responsibility both on the part of leadership and avant-garde intellectuals. Experiences of young Jews offering their own people's blood for "oil on the wheels of the revolution" have added to the fuel of antisemitism in Russia and in Poland. I suspect that attempts are being made to utilize the Negro plight, in a similar way, using the rationale which the social revolution that the white proletariat had not been willing to undertake in the 1930's will be successfully accomplished in the 1960's or 1970's with the Negro proletariat as a leader and integration as the mask. Jews have been used as the oil for the wheels of the revolution, both on the left and on the right. The accusation of undue Jewish participation in the communist movement had not only cost the Jews many victims, but has also furnished a potent anti-communist weapon to Hitler and his present and future emulators.

I well realize that some issues mentioned by me are not usually raised by Jewish spokesmen who meet with the Negro leaders.[17] Nevertheless, Jews do raise such questions that deserve a frank and honest Negro-Jewish dialogue. This cannot be achieved unless some Jewish spokesmen free themselves of their masochistic approach to their own people and Negro leaders begin to react to black racism as they would like to see white persons react to white racism. Regrettably, antisemitic and genocidal Negro extremists have been given respectability and recognition as leaders by

17 Worthy of note among more recent publications are the following: Cohen, Seymour J., *The Negro-Jewish Dialogue* (New York 1963) (Synagogue Council of America); Maslow, Will, "Negro-Jewish Relations in America," American Jewish Congress press release, Dec. 3, 1963; Polier, Shad, "The Jew and the Racial Crisis," *Congress Bi-Weekly* (Sept. 14, 1964), pp. 5-8; Podhoretz, Norman, "My Negro Problem—And Ours," *Commentary*, vol. xxxv (Feb. 1963), pp. 93-101; Shapiro, Manheim S., "The Negro Revolution—and Jews," *Council Woman* (April 1964), pp. 7-10; Sherman, C. Bezalel, "In the American Jewish Community. Negro and Jewish Relations," *Jewish Frontier*, vol. xxxi, no. 6 (July 1964), pp. 16-18; Syrkin, Marie, "Can Minorities Oppose 'De Facto' "Segregation," *ibid.*, vol. xxxi, no. 8 (Sept. 1964), pp. 6-12; Tartakower, Aryeh, "Problem of Negro Antisemitism," *Hadoar*, vol. xliv (Oct. 16, 1964), pp. 751-753; Weiss-Rosmarin, Trude, "Negro Antisemitism," *Jewish Spectator* (March 1964), pp. 3-4. The self-termed "progressive" *Jewish Currents* concentrates on integration as do organs of Jewish organizations, *e.g.*, *American Judaism, Congress Bi- Weekly, Midstream, The ADL Bulletin, The Committee Reporter, The Council Woman, The Reconstructionist.*—I have also benefitted from Mr. Asher S. Jacobs' assignment paper at Bernard Revel Graduate School, Yeshiva University, "Negro-Jewish Relations," May 1963.

legitimate Negro leaders and intellectuals. That is what happened to anti-semites in Germany, and the world is still paying for it. Responsible leaders should strive for the isolation of racists of any color and for their exposure as such. Negroes are a minority and can least of all afford to alienate the sympathy of the white majority by such tactics. The future of the Negro life in America depends, in a large measure, on the elimination of extremist racism.

A minority has the right to a certain amount of enlightened egotism. This goes for both Negroes and Jews. Wrong tactics in the struggle for equality can end very badly for all minorities.

I should like to close with a reassertion of the hope that the Conference on Jewish Social Studies and Negro academic institutions will be able to join forces and together help to shed light on our common problems.

APPENDIX

A Jewish Student's Reaction to a Radical Integrationist's Speech

Chicago, April 20, 1964

Last night Lawrence Landry spoke at—you guessed it—the Bernard Horwich Jewish Center. He is the fellow who plans the school boycotts here. Among other things he said that the civil rights bill is too late; this country is having a "black revolution"; there will be a stall-in here, just like the one in New York; the major northern cities will experience race riots until the Negro gets his "rights." He also complained about police brutality.—Needless to say, the Jews applauded. How about you? I'll reassure you, though. You don't have a car, so you have nothing to fear from a traffic jam. Of course, if there should be a fire, the fire department may have a wee bit of difficulty getting to the scene of the trouble. You're liberal and understanding, though. What does it matter if a few houses are burned and a few people roasted so long as the greater good—i.e. CORE, ACT, Landry, Adam Clayton Powell, Malcolm X, etc. etc. — are served? I wish I could be a liberal too, but unfortunately I am incapable of such magnanimous humanitarianism.

Until I had attended that foolishness, I, in the carefree optimism that can only be explained by my extreme youth, had believed that there was some hope for the Jewish people. I fear another fond illusion has gone by the boards. When I saw that rabble-rouser telling the Jews that they would suffer violence, lose their jobs, etc., and when the Jews applauded him, almost looking forward to the experience, I realize that this is a people that cannot forgive itself for existing, and is determined to change that status as quickly as possible. When Landry says that they must pay the price for three hundred years exploitation of the Negro, he has nothing to worry about. They'll pay an eternity's worth, and it won't diminish the Jewish feeling of guilt one bit. Were they that way in Europe too, or is this a new development?

The questions were insipid and stupid and obviously designed to make Mr. Landry look as right as right can be. I had my hand up the whole time but, needless to say, my question had not been scheduled and so I was never recognized. I suppose you've seen that happen on a number of occasions. Needless to say, an agitprop was present to lead the applause, and/or catcalls and derision when the names of President Johnson, Mayor Daley, or Martin Luther King were mentioned. They must have rehearsed for hours, but the stalwarts didn't have to. They couldn't have asked for a more responsive audience, or a more sympathetic one, for that matter. *Jüdischer Selbsthass.* [. . .]

HORACE MANN BOND'S RESPONSE

I was very interested in what Dr. Duker had to say. For example, he referred to the dismay members of the Jewish community might feel at the failure of Negro leaders to condemn the Black Muslims; he was also dismayed at the failure of the Negro community leadership to solve its own problems. I would like to say that under my passive, quiet and docile demeanor, I entertain an eating cancer in my subconscious or my conscious, and it's been there for sixty years. I have been mad all of this time. I have been frightfully angry at what was done to me and what was done to other Negroes, but for various reasons I maintained my placid surface and was nice to all people. I was a college president in Pennsylvania for a lot of years, and as a college president I was very pacific. You might call me a bitter, bitter man. For example, when you talk about the Negro leadership not condemning the Muslims, I thought of this picture I saw on T.V. last week of Msgr. Shean in his photograph with Gov. Wallace of Alabama whom I regard as one of the most immoral people in existence, and yet here was the great propagandist and converter for the Catholic Church showing every evidence of well-feeling and gentlemanly courtesy. I think Wallace is a sinner, an awful person. And although we say that Negroes are not faced with genocide, it seems to me, nonetheless, this is what has been going on all of the time. Sixty of every one thousand Negro babies born in Georgia die each year in their first year compared to about 25 of every thousand white children. And the same thing is true in New York. And this seems to me to be a kind of genocide that has been characteristic of the American system. Looking at it as a sin, as a wicked thing, I have this perverted feeling that all those who participate in this wickedness are themselves, wicked people. Do I make myself plain? And the degree to which the Negro people have been brutalized, these youngsters who jumped on the Jewish children up there, *are* inhuman, they *are* savages. But I say they were contrived to be made and manufactured as inhuman persons, and that is what the American system has done to the Negro people. Now I have revealed myself as a person who is really full of the same fundamental anger and frustration you read in James Baldwin's works and the rest of it.

I like Charles Silberman's suggestion that you start all of these children off in the third year in nursery school. I have proposed to my students in Atlanta University something much more radical than that and that is to go back to Plato's Republic and develop a school system in which the children who are born into a living hell from which they can never escape—a hell contrived by the American system—the only thing we can do for them is to create institutions in which you put them at infancy, away from the slum in which they are bound to be corrupted and brutalized and made into inhuman people. Mr. Silberman's suggestion may be a more practical thing than my conception of it.

I say it again, the whole system, and I see these children in Atlanta, and I can picture in my mind the attack upon Jewish children and I know the sort of children who do these acts. I say they are caricatures of the human capacity and were manufactured by the system in which we live. Those who have gone along with this system must bear partial responsibility for having connived and helped contrive this malformation of human beings: and do not expect the Negro leaders to do anything about this monstrous corruption of human beings.

I recently did a study in terms of my southern Congressmen on school expenditures (Russell, Talmadge and all of our Georgia Congressmen), working out some per capita figures for the Negro and the white children when they were in school. I found as you would expect, the amounts of money spent on the white children in their counties when these congressmen were children ran to some five to ten times as much as that spent on the Negro children. As a result you have all of these semi- or total Negro illiterates in New York City totally unprepared to cope with the world in which they now live; and on the contrary you have Mr. Russell who was educated by taking money that was appropriated for Negro children and then spent on him, now advocating a deportation of Negroes to various parts of the country. I say this with colossal rage and I generalize it. What I am talking about is that the human debris that accumulates in American cities in the Negro population, hurts me; but I don't want to take the responsibility for it because I did not make these people.

REMARKS BY DISCUSSANT LEO SROLE

I turn directly to Dr. Bond's presentation, which I found moving and informative, precisely because it was personal and anecdotal in nature. I agree with him, rather than with Dr. Duker, that the quality of antisemitic attitudes among Negroes, where they are present, tends to be rather different from those characterizing antisemitism among white Christians. There is an objective basis for the Negro's perception that he is oppressed in many areas of daily life and that whites are the oppressors. Jews are white and certainly share part of this guilt. Even more crucial, as Dr. Bond observed, is the fact that in Negro areas, Jews are conspicuous dispensers of housing, food, clothing and like basic creature needs, often with a sense of social responsibility incommensurate with the level of their economic interest in the Negro population. In Negro eyes, therefore, Jews they do business with represent the exploitive white society, functionally as well as symbolically. Consequently, the inevitable hostility, overt or covert, which Negroes bear towards whites and the white "system" is specially directed toward Jews. In this socio-psychological light, contemporary Negro antisemitism does not need the foundation in the Christian theological literature which Dr. Duker so heavily ascribes to it. In fact, I have the distinct impression that Negroes, more than other Christian groups, are strongly oriented to the Hebrew Bible because there they can identify themselves with Jews as one of the classical oppressed minorities in human history. Thus, their current attitudes toward contemporary Jews are often highly conflicted. And what Dr. Bond tactfully revealed to us today is that only recently have articulate Negroes like himself felt free to express the two sides of this conflict to Jewish audiences. I regret that Dr. Duker completely missed the point of Dr. Bond's candor.

Dr. Brotz has made a cogent analysis of certain psychological processes that are operating in the present situation. He did touch on one aspect that I want to comment on from my particular sociological perspective. The recent mobilization of Negroes in the civil rights struggle reflects more strikingly than ever the emergence of a significant middle class in the Negro population and, as a matter of fact, the existence also in the Negro community of a small wealthy upper class. I sometimes question how far most of them go in identifying themselves with the mass of economically deprived Negroes, but it is clear that without a relatively young, well-educated, militant segment of the Negro middle class, the civil rights struggle would never have acquired its organized strength and accelerating momentum.

Finally, I want to pick up a theme that Dr. Bond touched, namely the brutalizing, degrading impact of the whole discriminatory and segregating process in the American community. And here I can draw on my research of the past decade into sociological roots of psychopathology. Specifically, we have become aware of the fact that whosoever is the object of social disparagement and rejection suffers psychological wounds that stunt his development and cripple his capacity to actualize his inherent potentialities. This is true for individual deviants like the physically handicapped, and it is true when a whole group is branded with stigma and reviled as pariah, as are Negroes, and, to a somewhat lesser degree, as are poverty-level whites. Thus, when both of these groups are charged with lacking the energy and will for self-improvement, as I understood Dr. Brotz to imply about Negroes, we know that the matter is far more complicated than it sounds.

From recent community studies, such as are reported in Srole, Leo, *et al.*, *Mental Health in the Metropolis* (New York 1962), we are beginning to document that social stigmatization and segregation is destructive of the self. It drains energy; it kills motivation; it destroys self-confidence and the capacity for concentration and work. It produces crippled, twisted, apathetic, emotionally starved, defeated and self-defeating people. This is what we have found among poverty-level whites—and this is what we find among poverty-level Negroes; a psychological condition which corrodes their native strengths and capabilities to help themselves.

On the other side of the coin, I want to report a recent development that indicates where constructive energies and constructive solutions can be found. This is a report of an experiment that is being conducted in Chicago among young, largely illiterate, chronically unemployed Negroes who were welfare cases as were their parents before them. It so happened that the taxicab industry in Chicago had a shortage of drivers to replace those who had died and retired. Negroes, who had never before been able to get and hold a job, were intensively trained for jobs as taxicab drivers where they earned up to $100 weekly. The resulting transformation that has occurred in these previously problem-ridden people, in their self-respect, in their capacity to do things for themselves, to become respectable members of the community, has been simply astonishing. The lesson, I think, is clear. Democracy, in the sense of respect for the equal dignity and equal rights of every individual, is morally a categorical imperative. We can now add that it is also a categorical imperative for the psychological well-being of the individual and the sociological well-being of the community in all of its spheres.

THE CIVIL RIGHTS STRUGGLE

By Bayard Rustin

A great number of problems both in the Negro and in the Jewish community militate at this period against a great deal of affection between both communities at a grass roots level. We ought to face these problems very clearly and very honestly, if it is our real intention to make progress.

The first of these is the lack of empathy for the current Negro struggle on the part of a great number of Jewish people. Fundamentally, this lack springs from a tendency in the United States to oversimplify social issues. Let me illustrate. I have spoken with Jews recently who, without thought or understanding, immediately ask the following: "Why are Negroes raising so much sand? Why don't Negroes look to their problems internally as we did?" The chairman of the Parents and Taxpayers on the East Side in Yorkville told me at a meeting where we were having a debate, "Well you know, Mr. Rustin, the problem is I was born in a ghetto; I got out of it, I now own a Cadillac, I have my three children in college." Jews must first of all understand that no matter what problems they faced in this country, they faced them with a 5000-year history of a cult and a civilization behind them, with a history of family development which defied most family developments in the United States. Negroes, on the other hand, are burdened with a heritage of slavery, disruption of the family, and denial of rights. Also, the Jewish struggle against antisemitism and for American citizenship was fought simultaneously with the fight for trade unionism. But more significant is the fact that the Jewish development toward acceptance took place at a time of an expanding economy. But the Negro struggle takes place in a time of automation and cybernation. It takes place when, instead of economic expansion, which would make it possible for the Negroes, as some Jews say, "to lift themselves by their bootstraps," we have a reduction of jobs and economic opportunities. They cannot pull themselves up by their bootstraps. I reject even the Malcolm X claim that he is transforming prostitutes and dope addicts from being prostitutes and dope addicts into functioning citizens. This is not to say that he may not change one or two. But it is the closed ghetto which produces monstrosities—and I use these words advisedly—and for every prostitute or dope addict that Malcolm X thinks he has cured, the closed ghetto will make ten. Now here is something that Jews must under-

NB.

stand, namely, that they never faced a closed ghetto such as the Negro faces. First of all, they could change their name—and they could escape. The Negro has never had such avenues of escape. Hence for Jews to compare the closed ghetto with the ghetto they faced is a distorting oversimplification.

The second point is that the Negro people at this period have neither the economic nor the political power to solve their problems. There is ultimately no way to get jobs, housing and quality education with integration for Negroes unless many segments of this society which are not now in movement, join in movement. When we were dealing with public accommodations, it was possible for us to make considerable progress without anybody's help, because we were dealing only with segregation and discrimination. The tragedy of the Negro community at this moment is that it is formed to move when few others are in movement, especially the Jewish people, especially the trade union movement. Backed to the wall, in a situation of utter desperation, the Negroes are now forced not only to fight segregation and discrimination, but to fight the basic economic institutions of this country, if they are to have work. For to find work for Negroes in the time of automation means that Negroes and whites shall end up fighting in the streets over the few jobs, as the plumbers are doing. *Therefore the way out is not the civil rights revolution but the creation of an American revolution.* When the private sector of the economy cannot put men back to work, it is the responsibility of government to do so. We need planning in this economy, so that we may know what men can be trained for. President Johnson's effort at training men in a vacuum without planning is not only a lie, it is a hoax. We must have a 30 to 50 billion dollar works programs which will put men back to work. That is a program on which Negroes and whites can and must combine. Ten years after the Supreme Court decision, more Negroes are in segregated schools, in segregated housing, and without jobs than in 1954. This is a desperate situation.

Let me tell you about the incident near the Brooklyn Yeshiva. I will not excuse what happened. In a situation of this kind, in desperation, where no other segment of this society is prepared to move, Negroes will be desperate with everybody. And they will adopt as a slogan, "give everybody hell regardless of color or race or creed." When Jews think they are being singled out, that every little incident that occurs must be interpreted as some rise of Hitlerism, they understand neither the nature nor the complexity of the problem. For the people who believe that they must "give them hell regardless of race, color and creed" do not mean Jews first. They mean Roy Wilkins first and Jim Farmer first. They are tired, desperate, and fed up. In such a situation of desperation, not knowing what to do, they see people who look very queer and strange and who play no role which is understandable to them. These they will attack violently. They will also attack Negroes with whom they do not feel they have empathy. If you want to get to the bottom of what happened in Brooklyn, you need to remember that this is the way men behave when they are desperate. I, a pacifist who was opposed to all war and violence, have often publicly stated that I have nothing but complete respect for Jews who in the Warsaw ghetto rose up in arms. Why? Because in spite of my pacifism I have empathy enough to understand that men who have been forced into desperation must behave desperately. I do not mean to suggest that the Negro youth in Brooklyn had anything other than this in common with the fight in the Warsaw ghetto.

To my mind the greatest speech made at the March on Washington, historically, philosophically, was not Dr. King's, but Rabbi Prinz's, because Rabbi Prinz said something which makes a connection between the pecking system and double jeopardy. He said, "It is not the men who are evil and who behave in an evil manner. It is those who are silent." Now that combined two problems. If it is true that the Negroes engage in pecking, then it is also true that Jews in the South are involved in avoiding the problem out of the principle of double jeopardy. Which is worse? Both are evil. For I am here to tell you that the Jews in the South are playing no creative role in the struggle. When you think of what happens in Brooklyn or of antisemitism on the streets of Harlem, to which I am unalterably opposed and which I have fought and will fight, then you have to compare the sides, under the fear of double jeopardy, and cross it off with the pecking system which takes place here. Anybody in his right mind knows that as long as the Negro faces the frustration which he does, he will peck on somebody. This is a law of human behavior. The answer to both the double jeopardy and pecking lies in what Rabbi Prinz called "the courage to be open, the courage to fight."

Another great problem that is not a Jewish but an American problem, not a Negro, but an American problem, is that just as the N.A.A.C.P. lacks fundamental roots in the Negro community, so the Jewish organizations had better face the fact that they lack fundamental roots in their community. If that were not so, there would not be so many Jews in P.A.T. The problem here is that there is so broad a breach between (and I'm not only talking about Jews, now, I'm talking about NAACP and CORE, too), is that there is such a terrible breach between leadership and followership that we end up letting these people wallow because we do not give them real leadership. There is only one way to give them real leadership, and that is not by press releases, not by meetings, not by resolutions, but by joining the American struggle where it is taking place, in the streets. Let us get rabbis and ministers going out into the streets, not only for Negro rights. I, my friends, who was one of the first in the streets years ago, now know that, while we must stay in the streets for demonstrations, we have to stay in the streets simultaneously for a political program which will solve the problem. For no matter how many people lie in the streets to get jobs, lying in the streets is merely pointing out that jobs are needed. To produce jobs, one needs a political program in which the Negroes need allies. They need all religious groups, the best segments of labor, everyone, going into the streets, calling for ways of putting American workers back to work.

Finally, Jews are in a delicate and dangerous situation, as are all who stand for the right thing as a result of their history and out of their announced program. If you think the young fellows in CORE jump on Roy Wilkins and Jim Farmer and Martin King first because they dislike them, you are mistaken. In times of desperation, socially, you act like a child having a tantrum, a child saying, "watch me mother, I'm going to do something naughty, because I want you to come and show me a better way." After following Jim Farmer and Roy Wilkins and Rev. King, and all of the leaders, it is most likely that they will next jump on Jews who historically have been friendly to them. He who does not understand this, does not understand the psychology of people in motion. *Eat that Dukes*

ETHNIC AND RELIGIOUS MINORITIES: SUBCULTURES AND SUBCOMMUNITIES

By Ben Halpern

America has been reluctant to admit that it has ethnic or religious or any other kind of minorities. The American ideology holds that our nationhood, based on a *plébiscite de tous les jours,* derives directly from the individual citizen's pledge of allegiance to our political principles. Religion is irrelevant to it, race is irrelevant to it, and even culture, other than the specific civic culture of the Republic, is theoretically irrelevant to it. Just as there is no majority in belief, origin, or Old World traditions that is entitled to demand conformity to its values, so there can be, in principle, no religious, racial or ethnic minorities.

In fact, of course, there is a dominant group that feels entitled to demand conformity to its values; and while vaguely defined and variable in composition from issue to issue, there is a consensus of opinion which determines what kind of religion is approved and to what extent; what racial types are admitted to which positions; and what ethnic cultures are proper for which occasions. Accordingly, we have religious, racial, and ethnic minorities.

To the extent that American social science faces these facts, it seems to prefer dealing with them under some other categories than the terms "ethnic and religious minorities." Sociologists in particular prefer to talk of "subcultures" and "subcommunities."

The merit of the sociological terminology, from the American point of view, is that it stresses what is common rather than what is different. To be sure, terms like "subculture" and "subcommunity" suggest one aspect of conflict in the factual situation: namely the *subordination* of the minority culture and community to the majority. But their primary logical significance is the harmonious *inclusion* of the subculture and the subcommunity in the more comprehensive culture and community of the nation as a whole. This implication of the terminology faithfully expresses the standard American ideal. To relate it to the complex factual situation requires further exploration of the facts.

American Jews and Negroes are a particularly illuminating pair of cases for such exploration. They are both unquestionable minorities whose exclusion from generally shared values, rights and privileges, have been national issues; and their distinctive status and separation from other parts of the nation are not likely to disappear in the near future. In one case, that of the Jews, their separatism is legitimately founded on the American principle of the separation of church and state which recognizes the right of all religions to maintain values of the utmost seriousness peculiar to themselves. In the case of the Negroes, their segregation is a practice without sanction in the American ideology and with no value cherished by the Negroes themselves. Thus, while both Jews and Negroes are clearly minorities—in fact, classic American cases—it is less clear in what sense they can be subcultures and subcommunities.

Let us consider first how the conception "subculture" might apply to these two cases. In such a context, certain *prima facie* connotations of the term seem to be pertinent: a "subculture" implies values distinct from, subordinate to, and included under the dominant cultural values of the country as a whole. Using these criteria as a guide, students of the Negro and Jewish subcultures would be inclined to concentrate on such values as come under the heading of "folkways." The Negro subculture is likely to be conceived as a matter of jazz rhythms, blues notes and blues harmonies, spirituals and folksongs, fish fries and funerals and other touches of local color with which the Negro subcommunity, from Basin Street to Harlem, embroiders the basic fabric of American culture. The Jewish subculture would be considered a matter of a characteristic turn of wit and humor, derived from the *shtetl* and distilled and blended for the American market in the successive haunts of the Jewish subcommunity from the immigrant ghetto to the borscht belt to suburbia and exurbia; or it shows itself in relative immunity to alcoholism and addiction to higher education among Jews; and so on.

A subculture is conceived as a kind of experimental workshop in which small specialties are produced that can, if successful, be taken up into the general way of life of the nation as a whole. There is another implication: the serious and universal values of the American way of life, which make up our culture rather than our various subcultures, are not produced by the subcommunity. It is not often stressed who, in fact, does produce them—not since the open Know-Nothingism and nativism of earlier times. But any descriptive sociology would have to concede that our official *mores*, informal as well as formal, from the Puritan ethic and the ideal of rugged individualism to the Constitution, are produced primarily not by every American but by the majority: the white Anglo-Saxon Protestant community. This culture may be accepted, aquiesced in, or submitted to, by everybody; but the daily plebiscite that ratifies our national creed is, like every plebiscite, an enforced choice between alternatives which the electorate did not create but which are presented to them ready-made by their leaders.

One may ask, whether it is inevitable that the subcommunities should produce only such subcultural values as are acceptable to the nation as a whole; or whether, in fact, they do so. It is obvious that both qustions may be answered in the negative. Indeed, students of Jewish and Negro folk culture are inclined to decry those productions which become part of American mass culture as bowdlerized corruptions of authentic native folk creations. Also, the inner Negro or Jewish folk culture which does not gain general acceptance is by no means as blandly harmless to the national conventional values as the more familiar Negro and Jewish entertainment. This is by now generally recognized. There is a certain vogue in current literary criticism which recognizes Negro and Jewish writers as standard bearers of alienation, and regards Jewish, and especially, Negro (or Indian or Asian) figures in literature as symbolizing counter-conventional tendencies in Mark Twain, Herman Melville and other open or covert rebels. Morever, the current Negro revolution has lifted the curtain which veiled from general view the bitter feeling against the white majority pervading the inner Negro culture not produced for the general market.

If we turn again to the Jews, another question, less often faced, becomes pertinent. Is it inevitable that the subcommunity should accept the whole society; and does it in fact do so? The situation in America obscures the correct answers to one, at least, of these questions. That it is entirely possible for a subcommunity to reject values which the whole society regards as universally valid is a fact massively documented by centuries of Jewish life in exile.

Even today, despite the remarkable success of such formulas as "Judeo-Christian civilization" and Will Herberg's triple melting pot "Catholic-Protestant-Jew," the fact remains that the Jewish religious culture represents resistance to certain values which the dominant consensus regards as universally valid and, in effect, obligatory. The recurrent disputes over Bible reading in the public schools, Sabbath laws, and so on make this clear enough.

Thus the subcultures of both the Negro and Jewish subcommunities are far from being fully included in the general culture of the whole community; to a greater or lesser extent they stand in opposition to it. But this resistance is by no means the same thing in both cases. Indeed, without too much violence to the facts one could set them up as ideal types in polar opposition. In culture, conflict may be of two kinds, which I call mythic and ideological respectively.* If the conflict is only mythic, people can live within a consensus defined by the same ideology, and temper the strains of its rigidity by wit and humor and other ways in which disciplines can be relaxed or evaded without breaking them. If the conflict is ideological, there has to be a victory of one view, suppressing the other, or some compromise allowing of the coexistence of separate groups in opposition, with each living by its own distinct consensus.

---

* *See* my "The Dynamic Elements of Culture," *Ethics,* vol. lxv (July 1955), pp. 225-249.

The kind of group whose conflict with a majority culture remains on the *mythic* plane is exemplified by such types as serfs, slaves, pariahs, and other suppressed classes. When for fear of servile rebellions the master classes resort to violence against them, the aim is to put the lower classes back in their proper place; and when successful, the outcome is to keep them chained down. When there is peace between the masters and their bound men, the servile subcommunity keeps to its place as defined by the dominant culture and vents its resistance to suppression only in the veiled form of humor, games and other subcultural expressions. The masters, for their part, act the patron and care for the men bound to their person and their domain as their own people.

The kind of group whose conflict with a majority culture is *ideological* is exemplified by such types as religious sects, radical factions, and merchant adventurers. When the dominant community resorts to violence against them in fear of conquest or subversion, the aim is to expel or exterminate them, or to convert them to the ruling ideology; and, if successful, the outcome is to wipe them out as a subculture or subcommunity. When there is peace and tolerance between the dominant and dissident ideologies, the subcommunity lives partly or wholly outside the consensus of the main community and hence is regarded as in some degree alien. But as a loosely attached, mobile group it may occupy a relatively high social status in other respects, since it needs every advantage.

These are, of course, abstractions. It should not be expected that Jews or Negroes conform fully to either ideal type; and it would be far more normal that elements of both types should be found in the situation of any long established minority. But, allowing for such reservations, it is evident that American Negroes are as nearly as possible a case of the subcommunity whose subculture is purely mythic while the Jews are a case of the subcommunity whose subculture is ideological as well. If one considers not what each group would like to become and is now becoming, but what each group has been and the point from which each started, the distinction becomes particularly apposite. The Negroes were slaves but soon became Christians; they practically forgot, with rare exceptions, that they were ever anything but American. The Jews were free and unattached, and rose rapidly in wealth and position, but they remained unconverted and never really forgot their historic origins. The African reminiscences in the Negro's subculture only serve to ease the discomforts which his American values impose upon him. Jewish traditions, no matter how attenuated, never cease to set Jews at odds with certain basic values shared by all other Americans.

The differences between Jew and Negro are more apparent the more we look to the past. Today they are increasingly obscured, because the Negro is reaching for the benefits that attend the Jewish position while the Jew, for his part, hopes to attain some of the relative advantages of the Negro position. In his anxiety to be as purely American as the Negro is, the Jew reduces his ideological resistance as nearly as possible to the level of a mythic variant of general American culture. He thus weakens his independent consensus. The Negro, hoping to attain such a rise in status as the Jew has accomplished since immigration, heightens his opposition as nearly as possible to the level of ideology. This combativeness produces something like a Negro subcommunity organized around its own consensus, independent of the standards of the general American community.

The subcommunity in both cases makes an attempt to escape from the position it occupies *vis-à-vis* the larger American community. In neither case is it probable that this aim can be fully achieved.

An alienated subcommunity with an ideological subculture, like the Jews, can only end its conflict with the dominant community completely by abandoning its own and adopting the majority's ideology. American Jews today are an amalgam of associated individuals who have taken various positions towards these options. They range from orthodox Jews to atheists who function as Jews for only one reason: that they have not converted to Christianity.

For all their mutual opposition, all these form one community *vis-à-vis* the Gentile environment. Their own differences are significant enough to prevent the proper functioning of an independent consensus and the social controls necessary for effective internal discipline, such as Jews enjoyed traditionally. This symptom of disintegration, moreover, is welcomed by the greater part of American Jewry. They regard the ancient tradition of tight Jewish community organization as an encumbrance, for two reasons: some, precisely because the tradition is old and derived from the Old World; others, because they see in effective, united Jewish internal organization, consciously or not, a symptom and a symbol of Jewish ideological opposition to the majority culture. When Jewish community organization is reduced to the function of coordinating the undisciplined activities of its several component organizations, it seems to many Jews that this is an indication that the community has become less alien and more American.

The same motivation is evident in the strong drive to narrow the apparent distance between American Judaism and American Christianity and achieve further legitimation for Judaism in America. But here the inherent limits and self-defeating premises of this effort are evident.

Herberg's argument that Judaism is one of the three legitimate forms of American religion has a singularly ambivalent tone. If it were wholly true that all Americans had to be identified by religion, and Judaism were one of three accepted American identities, then it would be a striking success for Jewish social integration. This position involves the assumption that there is an underlying, primary American religion common to all three forms of American belief; and it also implies that the fundamental ties of Americans to their beliefs are not religious at all but social. Both implications are realized and regretted by Herberg. But mere regret is not an adequate response;

for if religion is to be taken seriously, it requires active rejection of American-ism as a religion common to its three subordinate religions and repudiation of the exploitation of church or synagogue as a mere cover for American belongingness. The truth is that all three religions have their independent ideologies and are not totally included in the American consensus; and, in the cases of Catholicism, and above all Judaism, independence means sig-nificant areas of conflict, implicit or explicit, with the dominant consensus.

The same conclusion must be drawn if we consider the current efforts to reduce the anti-Jewish potential of the Christian teachings concerning the crucifixion. It is quite clear that the new thesis concerning the Jews being proposed in Catholic circles alters nothing ideologically. If adopted, it would be an effort to contain the mythic consequences of Christian beliefs by more precise and sophisticated definition. Like the attempt to gain recognition for Judaism as one of three legitimate forms of American religion, this reform campaign clearly exposes its inherent limitations. The real aim in both cases is to achieve peaceful coexistence. In the case of the crucifixion issue, there is no pretense that peace will imply total inclusion, for the new theses quite openly leave Catholicism and Judaism in their traditional rivalry while re-stricting the armaments of their conflict.

Similar reflections are in order about the current Negro revolution. It probably cannot alter the fundamental position. Some methods it employs seem to imply that such a goal is attainable, but their effect is inherently limited and in some respects opposite to the professed aim.

The Negro community seeks to overcome its unfreedom in two ways: by conquering a status comparable to that of the Jews; and by forcing on the dominant culture a revision of values such as the Jews would never dream of attempting. Given the Negro situation, here is an inherent connection between these two aims. An ideologically organized suppressed class can only achieve a rise in its status by revising the whole accepted scale of values that assigns it an inferior social position.

There are two conceivable ways in which this aim could be sought. Each runs into its own roadblock, and leads to a success rather different from the original intention. The Negroes at the present time are groping along both ways simultaneously without a clear view of the end of the road.

When a group bound to an inferior position in society becomes rebelli-ous, the battle itself produces an active ideological consensus among them. Their subculture, which formerly functioned as a safety valve for resentments and facilitated their submission, now asserts its own values independently and begins to establish the group's inner discipline. Taken to its conclusion, the way of independent group consciousness could conceivably achieve an im-proved status for the Negroes while short-circuiting their rebellion. Negro nationalism, the People of Islam and similar separatist movements are un-doubtedly foremost among the expressions of sheer anti-white protest; but by fostering self-reliance and self-discipline in the Negro community they could also indirectly overcome some considerable obstacles to Negro social and economic advancement. Not only the Jews and Chinese, or the Huguenots, but, as Nathan Glazer has noted in some detail, also the Puerto Ricans find that the heightened mobility and solidarity of a separatist minority aid them to rise in the social scale. The Negro separatist movements, for their part, already point to the heightened morale and social effectiveness they produce among their adherents.

Separatism as a Negro tactic means, however, abandoning the hope that the Negro rebellion will succeed by altering the value patterns of the entire white community. However rebellious in origin, it is objectively a method suited to a group that is reconciled to remaining a minority. It is quite reasonable that Malcolm X should have left the Black Muslims in order to get deeper into the Negro revolution. Only the Negro civil righters have a goal which requires them to revolutionize all white society and offers no shortcut to racial peace.

Ideological separatism is likely to produce only minor cults among the Negroes. The reason for this is neither that separatism is radically rebellious in mood nor that it is moderately realistic in its longrun effects, but that the success of an ideological movement usually depends on the inherent appeal of its ideology. Social conflict may compel a group to develop its own independent consensus for the sake of the battle, but it is not enough to produce an integrated culture. The general American culture holds such unquestioned dominance in the minds of American Negroes that cultural independence can appeal inherently to only a few marginal groups.

James Baldwin reminds us of the essential nature of the Negro rebellion with his constant impassioned outcry that the American Negro is no more than a myth created by the whites. This view merits the explication of some of its facets and implications. If the Negro is a myth, then he has been created not only by the whites but also by the Negroes themselves and with a strangely similar intent. The American ideology of liberty and freedom for all, without distinction of race, creed and so on, cannot be lived with in total compliance; no more so than any pure ideal. The myths may perpetuate, but they do not create, the discordance between fact and ideal, so that we could hope that destroying the myth would realize the ideal. Whites create a myth of the Negro to justify their departure from ideological purism; Negroes, in submissive resentment, shape their subculture into a countermyth that serves the same purpose for them. The present Negro rebellion, at some levels, takes the form of proposing the elevation of a Negro countermyth into an independent ideological principle upon which the Negro community could build its separation. But for most Negroes, and their leadership, there is no inherent appeal in the Negro subculture powerful enough to make them take this line. They are thrown back on a neo-orthodoxy of Americanism, on an ideology of iconoclasm which wishes to do without myth and rebuild American society on bare principles.

As a revolutionary slogan, this has its effectiveness. The cultural justification for the inferior position of American Negroes is a myth crude enough to repel any American liberal with a vestige of puritanical rigor. The Negroes are a minority relatively so small and weak that they depend on the support they can expect from guilty white consciences. But as a constructive principle, sheer anti-mythic iconoclasm is blindly unrealistic. Myths create facts far less effectively than facts evoke myths. What has to be overcome is not the Negro myth but the Negro position; and sheer idealism simply will not do the job. One may add that in the very fight to destroy the Negro myth, the Baldwins are building a consciousness of kind and a group morale among Negroes which, in rudimentary form, are the prerequisites for an organized, self-maintaining community.

Starting from opposite ends, the Jewish and Negro subcommunities have converged on the same point, and face the same difficulty, though they may hope for solutions which will again diverge. The Jews are losing their internal discipline and distinct ideological consensus, and remain an alienated subcommunity for reasons which are more and more mythic. The Negroes are being brought by their current revolution to a pitch of communal discipline and ideological consensus that make them a subcommunity increasingly alienated and not just suppressed; but their subculture has little in it to uphold an ideological distinctiveness. Alienation without enough cultural substance to justify it is not only a dull but an unstable form of communal existence. It may be propped up indefinitely by circumstances but cannot be enjoyed and cherished. The constant strain to escape it is inescapable. But while many Jews would hope they can escape it by reclaiming their cultural distinction, many Negroes would hope for a redemption that totally erased their difference.

THE MERCHANT AND THE LOW-INCOME CONSUMER

By David Caplovitz

A strategic place for examining relationships between Jews and Negroes is the world of commerce where the Jew is typically the merchant and the Negro the customer. Leaders of both communities have warned that this is an area in which the interests of the two groups come into conflict and strains between them have developed. Unfortunately, I cannot shed much light on the degree to which Jewish-Negro relations have been impaired by what happens in the marketplace since the study I will report on did not go into this matter. The title of my paper is deliberately broader than the theme of this conference. I could have entitled it, The Relations Between Jewish Merchants and Lower-Class Negro Consumers, without doing too much harm to the data, since many, if not all, of the merchants I will describe happen to be Jews and many of the customers are Negroes. But I have chosen the more general title for several reasons. First the marketing relationship I will describe is not limited to Jewish merchants and Negro customers. The important elements in this relationship are the low income and low education of the customers, whatever their color, and how the merchants adapt to and, I might add, take advantage of, these facts. A second reason for the more general title is related to a basic weakness of my study from the viewpoint of the theme of this conference. Although I can tell you about the *behavior* of lower-class Negroes as consumers and about the practices of Jewish merchants who supply them with the goods they want, I have virtually no information on the all important question of how the Negroes *perceive* the merchants with whom they deal as Jews. In short, I cannot tell you how the strains and tensions that can and do develop in this economic relationship have affected the attitudes of Negroes toward Jews.

The study to which I referred grew out of the efforts of three settlement houses in New York City to do something about the consumer problems of the poor people in their neighborhoods.* In 1960, these settlements commissioned the Bureau of Applied Social Research of Columbia University to carry out a survey of the consumer practices of low-income families as a

*For a full account of this study *see* my *The Poor Pay More* (New York 1963).

prelude to a program of action. Two of these settlements were located in East Harlem and one on the Lower East Side. In all, we interviewed 464 families living in low-income public housing projects in these two areas. In order to get the merchants' views of the marketing situation, we carried out more informal interviews with some of the many merchants of furniture and appliances located in East Harlem, along 3rd Avenue and 125th Street. The density of furniture and appliance stores in this area is probably greater than anywhere else in the country.

The median income of the families we interviewed was about $3,300 in 1960, the year of the study. Most of them were members of racial or ethnic minorities. Forty-five percent were Puerto Rican, 30 percent Negro and 25 percent white, exclusive of Puerto Ricans. Relatively few, only 17 percent, were natives of the city. The rest were migrants, generally from the South or from Puerto Rico. Their educational level was quite low. Only 17 percent of the family heads had completed high school and about half did not continue their education beyond grade school.

Their place of origin, their ethnicity, their low educational level, all suggest that these consumers are products of more traditionalistic cultures, poorly trained in the ways of urban, bureaucratic society. This fact underlies many of the problems they encounter as consumers.

Consumer Practices of the Poor

We might suppose that families whose incomes average only about $3,300 could not possibly be consumers of expensive durable goods. But this reasoning overlooks that rapidly expanding American institution, the installment plan and the special forms it takes in low-income areas. "No-money-down" and "easy payments" are the slogans luring even the poor into the marketplace. Our survey disclosed that in spite of their poor economic position and poor credit status, most of the families were consumers of major durables. For example: 95 percent owned at least one televesion set (5 percent owned more than one); more than 3 in every 5 owned a phonograph; more than 2 in every 5 owned a sewing machine; more than 2 in every 5 owned an automatic washing machine; more than a quarter owned a vacuum cleaner; one in every 7 families owned an automobile.

Most of the families had moved into public housing during the five-year period preceding the study, and most of them had bought a good deal of furniture in that period. The typical family bought sets of furniture for at least two rooms when it moved into the project and had spent approximately $500. Some 16 percent had paid more than $1,000 for furniture bought at the time of the move. The prices they paid for appliances were quite high. Forty percent paid more than $300 for their TV set and 13 percent paid more than $400. A number of families owned expensive combination television and phonograph sets and one family reported paying $900 for such an appliance.

It is not surprising that these families relied heavily on installment credit when making such expensive purchases. Approximately two-thirds of the appliances owned by the families were bought on credit and 80 percent had used credit to buy at least some of their major durables. Their dependence on credit and their traditionalistic backgrounds account for the fact that hardly any shopped for major durables in the downtown department stores and discount houses. They went instead to the local stores or to the appliance chain stores that advertise "easy credit" plans.

It may come as a surprise to learn that the door-to-door peddlers, the men with the traditional slogan of "a dollar down, a dollar a week," are still thriving among the poor, finding new customers among the more recent migrants from the rural South and Puerto Rico.

Fully half the families we interviewed had made at least one credit purchase from these door-to-door salesmen, and more than a third had made repeated purchases. Most families regretted buying this way when they discovered they were paying exorbitant prices. But some, approximately 20 percent, have had rather continuous relationships with peddlers, whom they have come to regard as almost a friend. The peddler serves as a purchasing agent for these families, getting them practically anything they need. Unlike most of the local merchants and the more bureaucratic stores that offer credit, most of the peddlers do not use installment contracts. The exceptions are outdoor salesmen for large firms specializing in a particular commodity such as encyclopedias or pots and pans. These men are not interested in building up a clientele. Once the contract is signed, this kind of salesman gives the customer a coupon book with instructions for mailing monthly payments, and then he disappears. But the more usual peddler is the man in business for himself, hoping to establish permanent relationships with his customers. His credit is of a more traditional kind. When payments are late or are less than the specified amount, he does not add on service charges. This flexibility is appreciated by the customers and explains why some continue to buy from peddlers even though they know they pay much more than they would at a store.

It would be of great interest to know whether the occupation of customer-peddler (as these salesmen call themselves) is still dominated by Jews as it was in the early decades of the century. Although I cannot give you any statistics on this, my guess is that a majority of the peddlers today, particularly those in business for themselves are Jews, but that a growing number of Puerto Ricans are also playing this role. However, I suspect that most of the Puerto Rican peddlers are outdoor salesmen for one or another of the local stores. At least I make this inference from the fact that many of the stores in East Harlem have signs in their windows announcing the need for Spanish-speaking canvassers.

Consumer Problems and Patterns of Exploitation

Their lack of shopping sophistication and their vulnerability to "easy credit" would suggest that many low-income families encounter serious difficulties as consumers. The study found this to be true. One in every five had experienced legal pressures because of missed payments. Their goods were repossessed, their salaries were garnisheed or they were threatened with garnishments. Many of the families in this position had heavy credit obligations that reached crisis proportions when their income was suddenly reduced through illness or unemployment. The following account given by a 27-year-old Negro husband is typical:

> I first bought a bedroom set. I still owed money on it when I wanted a living room set. I went back to the store and bought the living room set on credit. *At that time I was working and making good money. That was two years ago. Six months ago I got sick and stopped working. And so I couldn't pay anymore* . . . When I got sick, I still owed $288. Last week they sent a summons saying I have to pay $440, not $288. We have to pay, but what I'm going to do is pay the $288, not the $440.

 Like many of these consumers, this young man did not understand that he is liable for the interest on his debt as well as court costs and legal fees.

Inability to maintain payments was not the only problem these consumers encountered. A much larger proportion—almost half of the sample—encountered difficulties because of the unethical and illegal practices employed by the merchants. This group includes families who were seduced by "bait advertising" and high-pressure salesmen into buying much more expensive merchandise than they had intended to buy, families who were given erroneous information about the costs of their purchases and families who were sold as new, merchandise that had been reconditioned.

The many incidents of "bait advertising" uncovered in the study can be illustrated by this typical experience of a 26-year-old Negro housewife:

> I saw a TV ad for a $29 sewing machine, so I wrote to the company and they sent down a salesman who demonstrated it for me. It shook the whole house, but I wanted to buy it anyway. But he kept saying it would disturb the neighbors by being so noisy and he went out into the hall and brough in another model costing $185. . . . I actually had to pay $220. He promised if I paid within a certain amount of time I would get $35 back. But since my husband was out of work, we couldn't pay within the time period, so I didn't get the refund. . . . I was taken in by the high-pressure sales talk.

It should be noted that these high pressure techniques often result in converting cash customers into credit customers. People who have every intention of paying cash when they answer the advertisement for the cheaper item suddenly find themselves buying much more expensive merchandise on credit.

The great success merchants have with "bait advertising" is indicated by the remarks of one of the furniture salesmen to whom we spoke in East Harlem: "I don't know how we do it. We advertise three rooms of furniture for $149 and the customers swarm in. They end up buying a $400 bedroom set for $600 and none of us can believe how easy it is to make these sales." The technique of persuading the customer to buy items more expensive than those advertised is known in the trade as "the switch sale," and judging from this account such sales are not hard to come by. Another merchant told us that the amount of goods sold a customer depends more on how much risk the merchant is ready to assume than on the buying intentions of the customer. The merchant ready to assume great risk can presumably persuade the low-income customer to buy more than he intended to buy when he first entered the store.

I am sure that the proportion of families who are victimized by unscrupulous salesmen is much greater than our study uncovered, simply because many of these families do not realize that they have been cheated. This discovery is often made by accident. For example, a family may learn that it was sold a reconditioned TV set only when so informed by the repairman, or they may learn from a friend that a particular item could have been obtained elsewhere for much less. Occasionally one of these consumers would learn that he was overcharged by having an item appraised. One middle-aged Negro housewife told us that she agreed to buy her daughter a watch that a door-to-door salesman was selling for $60. "I gave him $3 down and got a payment book in the mail. About a month later I had the watch appraised in a 125th Street store and I found it was worth only $6.50." This woman tried to break the contract but did not succeed. When she stopped payments the company sued her and won a judgment by default.

As this incident indicates, the two kinds of problems that low-income consumers encounter—failure to maintain payments and being victimized by the sharp practices of the merchants are not necessarily independent of each other. Some families, capable of maintaining payments stopped paying when they discovered that they had been cheated. But instead of gaining retribution, they were more often than not subjected to legal sanctions brought upon them by the merchant. This process can be seen in the experience of a 28-year-old Puerto Rican man:

> I bought a set of pots and pans from a door-to-door salesman. They were of very poor quality and I wanted to give them back but they wouldn't take them. I stopped paying and told them to change them or take them back. I refused to pay. . . They started bothering me at every job I had. Then they wrote to my current job and my boss is taking $6 weekly from my pay and sending it to pay this.

It is not clear from his account whether he had lost some of his previous jobs because of the efforts to garnishee his salary; this does happen with some frequency. Many employers simply will not be bothered with garnishments and do not hesitate to fire workers whose salaries are attached.

As the previous incident suggests, the laws regulating installment sales unwittingly act in favor of such merchants, because these poor consumers have little understanding of their legal rights and how to exercise them. By taking matters into their own hands and stopping payments on faulty merchandise, they only bring additional troubles upon themselves.

There is another aspect to this unwitting bias in the legal structure. The merchants who offer "easy credit" frequently sell their contracts at a discount to a finance company. Many low-income consumers do not understand this procedure. They mistakenly believe that the merchant has gone out of business and assume that nothing can be done about their problem. The practice of selling contracts to credit agencies thus often has the consequence of absolving the merchant of his responsibilities to the consumer, not because the law gives him this right, but because the consumer does not understand what has happened.

In keeping with their inadequacies as consumers in a bureaucratic society, most of the poor families we spoke to had no idea of what they could do about their consumer problems. When asked directly where they would go for help if they found themselves being cheated by a merchant, some 64 percent said they did not know. They could not name any of the community agencies equipped to deal with these problems, such as the Legal Aid Society, the State Banking and Finance Department, the Small Claims Court, or the Better Business Bureau. The Better Business Bureau was the agency most often cited by the minority who had some idea where they could go for professional help.

The Low-Income Marketing System

As I noted earlier, we interviewed some of the merchants in East Harlem and I will conclude this review of our study by giving you a brief picture of the techniques they employ to insure that the business will be profitable in spite of their readiness to extend credit to relatively poor risks.

Some of the incidents I have cited suggest one way in which the merchants protect themselves and that is to have unusually high markups on their merchandise. In this special system of sales-and-credit, cheap goods are sold at prices that in the larger market place are commanded by high quality merchandise. In East Harlem, one of the areas studied, the merchants use a number system to price their goods, referring to "one number," "two number" and "three number" items. Each number stands for a 100 percent markup over the wholesale price. For example, a TV set that costs the merchant $100 and is sold for $300 is a "two number" item. According to a former bookkeeper in such a store, the merchandise in East Harlem is never sold for less than one number and often for more. Another sign of an unusual pricing system in these stores is the absence of price tags, signifying that prices are not standardized; there are hardly any "one price" stories in low-income neighborhoods.

But the high markup does not in itself insure that the business will be profitable. No matter what he charges the merchant can stay in business only if he receives payments from his customers. The assumptions of any credit system—the customer's intention and ability to pay—cannot be taken for granted in this market.

To some extent the merchant can count on legal controls over his cus tomers. But these often prove inadequate, since many of the customers are employed only irregularly and others depend on welfare. Furthermore, the merchant who frequently resorts to legal controls is likely to lose good will in the neighborhood. For this reason, the merchants interviewed were reluctant to make extensive use of their right to sue defaulting customers.

Thus, in addition to formal controls, the merchants depend heavily on informal, personal controls over their customers. The merchants reported that they operate their credit business on a "fifteen-month year," anticipating that their customers will miss about one in every four payments. This is considered a normal part of the business and the merchants take it into account when they compute the markup.

Many merchants adopt the methods of the customer peddlers, employing their own canvassers who visit the families in their homes, both to collect payments and to sell additional merchandise. As part of the informal system of control, the merchants encourage weekly payment plans with the customer bringing the payment to the store. This continuous contact enables the merchant to get to know his customer. He learns when the customer receives his pay check, when his rent is due, when job layoffs, illnesses, and other emergencies occur; in short, he gathers all kinds of information that allow him to interpret the reasons for a missed payment. Since the customer comes to the store with his payments, the merchant is ready to make another sale when the first is almost paid for. As a result, many customers are continuously in debt to the merchant in a pattern reminiscent of the relationship between the sharecropper and the company store. We might almost call these traditionalistic consumers in our cities "urban sharecroppers."

Various devices are employed in this marketing system for sifting and sorting the consumers according to their risk and matching them with merchants willing to extend them credit. For example, when a merchant finds himself with a customer he considers to be too great a risk for him, he does not discourage the customer. Instead he directs him to a merchant with a less conservative credit policy. The peddlers also steer their customers to local merchants. When their customers request major appliances that they do not handle themselves, the peddlers will refer them to an appropriate merchant who is ready to extend them credit. The referring merchants and peddlers receive a commission for their service, another factor affecting the final sales price.

In describing what I call the low-income marketing system, I have stressed the inequities in this system of exchange, its exploitative features. But how is the persistence of such a deviant social system to be explained? Is it merely a matter of evil merchants taking advantage of the gullible poor? I think the answer is more complicated. This system with its obvious exploitative practices is able to persist because it performs important social functions. In a society in which consumption is not only a matter of obtaining material conveniences, but also a means of gaining self-respect and winning the respect of others, this marketing system makes consumers of the people who fail to meet the requirements of the more legitimate economy. Even the welfare family is able to consume in much the same manner as its social peers who happen not to be on welfare. Through the various mechanisms I have mentioned, the poorest risks are shunted to the merchants who are ready to accept great risk. A close association probably exists between the amount of risk that merchants in this system are willing to accept and their readiness to employ unethical and illegal tactics. It may even be that under the present marketing arrangements in our society, unethical practices are an inevitable consequence of serving the wants of the poorest risks. Society now virtually presents the poor risks with the unpalatable choice of foregoing major purchases and thereby forfeiting whatever self-esteem is to be derived from consumption, or being exploited. In short, the behavior of the local merchants must be seen in the broader context of a society in which even the poor are conditioned to want durable goods as a way of gaining self respect.

What relevance does this 1960 study have for the theme of this conference? As I noted at the outset, most of the merchants in the low-income marketing system I have described are Jews, and many of their customers are Negroes. It is quite possible then, that Negroes develop antisemitic sentiments when they discover that they have been victimized by salesmen and merchants they know to be Jews. The potential for such an outcome is certainly present. But it is a mistake, I think, to assume that this is the only outcome of the relationship between Jewish merchants and Negro customers. In the exploratory stages of our study I recall interviewing a young Negro who kept referring to his friend who owned an appliance store and from whom he bought the appliances he needed. We later learned that this particular store employed many outdoor salesmen, and my guess would be that this young man's friend was such a canvasser. It is of some interest that the salesmen are sometimes viewed as friends. I suspect that a more thorough study might show that the poor often turn to the merchants with whom they deal for a variety of services apart from merchandise. In the cold, impersonal bureaucratic world with which they have difficulty coping, the poor may consider the merchants as their allies. In calling attention to this other side of the "exploitative" relationship, I have no intention of excusing the sharp practices employed by the merchants. Just as I suspect that the patterns of exploitation are not to be explained on the grounds of man's evilness, so I suspect that the merchants' acts of friendliness toward their customers stem more from the desire to build good will than from innate altruism.

In stressing the impersonal forces shaping the behavior of the merchants vis-à-vis the poor consumer, I do not mean to imply that the abuses of this marketing system must be accepted as inevitable. Ways must be found through legislation and education for making the merchants more responsible for their actions. The exploitative features of this marketing system cannot possibly reflect favorably upon the Jewish community. The strains in the present system, I fear, will only be heightened as the Negro community becomes more self-conscious of its rights and more dissatisfied with the status quo. But I am not too optimistic about the possibilities of correcting these abuses through ethical appeals to the merchants. It is not an easy task to convince businessmen—whatever their ethnic origin or religion—to lower their profits in the name of ethical and humanitarian standards.

REMARKS BY DISCUSSANT CLEVELAND ROBINSON

I must start by making clear that I am from a trade union, District 65 where we take pride in the fact that over the years we have developed unity amongst all our members, Negro and white, Jew and Gentile, and have blended together a force for good. We are a fighting union.

Both Negroes and Jews are numerically a minority in our union, but our union was formed by a group of Jewish immigrants under the leadership of its first president, Arthur Osman who is now an international representative. I say that because it was through the work of this group of Jewish immigrants that District 65 grew and became a home for oppressed people, Negro, Puerto Rican as well as others. A policy was evolved which took into account all the problems which these oppressed peoples faced. The union became an instrument within which these groups could fight oppression. Hence, not only the Jews use the machinery of the union to articulate problems which are close to their hearts, whether in this country, Europe or Israel—but also Negroes, Irish, Italians and now Puerto Ricans. This came about because of the vision and wisdom of the Jewish leadership which founded this union. When we discuss the relationship of Jews and Negroes in the labor movement, it is important to emphasize what could have been done but was not, as well as what has been done.

I do not want anyone to misinterpret what I say as reflecting indifference to antisemitism. Through work in the labor union movement, I have been known as a fighter against antisemitism not just by words but by actions. The crisis which we face in our nation today is often interpreted in terms of the Negro revolution. However, I see something much larger than that. It may be because the Negro, oppressed as he was for so long, is manifesting that oppression in visible forms for all America to see. But working people in America are facing a crisis and this is not made sufficiently visible. At an executive board meeting of our international some months ago we had a discussion about collecting money for political action. We considered what the John Birch Society and similar organizations were doing. A gigantic campaign is going on throughout the country. One organization alone, I think, has some 422 radio stations at its command, another has 128. If you will get to the bottom of it, this campaign is basically fascistic, anti-Negro, anti-Jewish, anti-workers. There is developing in this nation, in my belief, a frightening spectacle. What troubles me is that the labor movement as a whole and progressive people, including Jews, do not seem to see this. Or if they do see it, they probably believe that by remaining silent it will pass over their heads. I think this is the basic problem we face.

When we discuss the relationship of Jews and Negroes, I cannot talk with much authority about the nation as a whole. I hold some international positions; I am an International Vice President of my international union, I am a National Vice President of the Negro American Labor Council which we founded under the leadership of A. Philip Randolph in 1959 or 1960. It was basically founded by Negro workers in order to combat discrimination in the labor movement, as well as in industry and government. But I note just what happens around us in our Northern communities and I know what happens in the City of New York. I owe it to you to tell what happens; what our Negro people, Negro workers are saying in the community and how they feel and how they react.

The last speaker mentioned the fact that nobody took the plumbers union for a Jewish union. Well, that may be so among the Jewish community, but in the Negro community this is said day by day. Certain names are synonomous with Jewish people. When the president of the plumbers union whose name is Mr. Cohen does not appear and it is published in the papers, Negro workers of course know he is a Jewish president. So it has a very bad impact. The fact that some great unions such as the Amalgamated, the I.L.G.W.U.—fine unions with rich histories—are today under criticism in the Negro community should be known and understood. I do not want to detract from what these unions have done in the past. The fact is that today Negro workers are at the bottom of the economic ladder if they happen to be in these unions. Their wages are very low. In too many instances they do not share the jobs which are on top. Too often the excuse for not fighting for higher wages is that these companies will leave town. The Negro workers look about and see white workers, including Jewish workers, enjoying the high-skilled wages while even when the Negro workers are skilled they still have no chance for promotion.

We talk about the building trades, but do not think it is in the building trades alone that the Negro community has complaints. We have it in the industrial unions also.

I am here as secretary-treasurer of my union and have mentioned the fact that I am International Vice President. The fact is that there are not many unions with Negro leadership of this stature. This would indicate that not only do the Negroes not share in the available jobs but also that they do not share in the leadership. This is one of the grievances that is prevalent in the Negro community. These things should have been looked into but were not. When one talks about the fact that there are feelings and tendencies in the Negro community which could be described as anti-semitic, I think that these matters must be taken into consideration. I will go further. Many of the employers in industrial plants are Jewish. Too often they have contracts which could be described as "sweetheart contracts." These contracts keep wages at the bottom—if the minimum wage is $1.25, these workers get $1.25. In too many instances, to get their jobs, they have to pay an agency fee. When they begin working, they pay the initiation fee, and as soon as the agency fee and the initiation fee have been paid, many of these workers are out of a job. The season is over and next season, they are never recalled. Such are some of the problems we face. Therefore, I think we ought to find ways to correct these situations for as I said earlier, we do face a crisis where the working people, black and white, need to unite in order to fight the collossal giant which I see rising up in the form of the Birchites and their associates who will destroy not only the Negro but both the Negro and the Jew.

Now, frequently, one will hear that this situation exists in many unions. This is true. In some unions which do not have Jewish leadership, it is worse. Negroes sometimes are not even admitted. But I believe that in to-day's market we have a situation which I might describe as follows: When we talk about the liberal community, the term "liberal" may be omitted as far as I am concerned and we would be talking about the same people, because the Jewish community has been most progressive, most liberal— has always been out there fighting. In the last several years a polarization has taken place between the Negro community and this community. There is the feeling that this liberal community does not understand the feelings and problems of the Negro community. Bayard Rustin today was quite correct when he pointed this out, and we have to draw some very im-portant lessons from it.

In our Negro community there are people who have been beaten down, denied jobs or given the worst ones, people who have been denied educa-tion, been walled in, caged in like animals, and this generation after gen-eration. Any sociologist will tell you that if you treat a human being like an animal, he will become like an animal. Negroes so treated are not prone to follow the advice of those leaders who are saying "be patient." This is true among the younger Negroes. They just can't understand. They now read a little more than their elders did. They know a little better than their elders knew and they want the things they read about. And there is no way in the world to tell them they cannot have them. They are prepared to die for them. And basically they see no difference in dying for them here or on some distant battlefield. I tell you frankly as one who has worked diligently with all groups, Negro, white, Gentile, I have many troubled moments because too often I do not seem to communicate the feelings I see expressed in the Negro community. I think there is misunderstanding in the white community. Instead of having both the Negro and white community realize the dangers we face, namely that fascism is knocking at our doors and that we have to join hands and fight, they are more likely to be fighting each other. Perhaps things have to get worse before they can get better, but I pray to God that they do not. The trade union movement has a grave responsibility. To the extent that those in the trade union leadership who are Jews do not speak out and act in a manner to move the trade union movement forward, to that extent they are guilty. It is ironic that today the President of the United States is the most progressive force in the country. Check on every piece of progressive legislation or action and see whether the labor movement is ahead or behind the President. You will find in every instance the labor movement is behind, not ahead. What we need is a labor movement and a progressive community calling for things which the President of the United States is not ready to give or because he is faced with pressures from the right, but the pressure of the people will move him.

On the question of what the Negro community is doing to cement relationships between the Negro and Jewish community, I should say that some in the Negro community are not much concerned about such a unity because they feel that the white community does not care. They are more concerned with mobilizing the Negro community to do battle. I think this must be put on the record. Others feel that unity is necessary and that we need to move together. But there are difficulties because the leadership which expresses the need for unity, for moving together, finds its hands tied for the reason that the white community, by and large, is not prepared to move and because the Negro community looks upon that leadership as if it were holding things back.

 I have to deal with people in my community day by day and I know the fears that exist. I can truly speak to them about antisemitism, but it runs like water off a duck's back because they can cite by chapter and verse whose foot is on their necks. Then I ask myself, "How do I cope with this in my community?" Should there not be some way people and some organizations whose work can be pointed out as belying the foot-on-our-necks idea? For example, in the labor movement, the struggle of the hospital workers is known. Leon Davis happens to be a Jew even though he was sentenced to six months by a Jewish judge but he continued that fight. He consulted with Dave Livingston of District 65, and both unions and their memberships went all out to relieve the sufferings of tens of thousands of hospital workers, 90 percent Negro and Puerto Rican. This is an example which I can show, but it is not enough. We have to face that fact. What happened in the Jewish community is that it has moved up the ladder and may of its members are comfortable and think they should not jeopardize their position. This is why I pointed to the danger of fascism which will destroy both Jews and Negroes. I say to you it has gone beyond the war on poverty. The real question is this: what kind of an America are we going to have?

REMARKS BY DISCUSSANT MORRIS U. SCHAPPES

As Prof. Halpern pointed out at the Luncheon Session, the Conference on Jewish Social Studies, in arranging our discussion today, had a duty both of commitment and detachment.

As a Jewish survivalist, I should say that I am committed to the struggle for Negro equality as part of the struggle for the democracy needed also for Jewish group survival, and I seek the detachment required for social science in order to refine and improve the effectiveness of my commitment.

My commitment is that of a secular Jew, for I am not a religious Jew. The record shows that the activity of secular Jews in this current struggle for Negro equality goes back for several decades — at least to the Scottsboro Case in the 1930's. Reporting on "New Jewish Initiatives in the Field of Race" to the National Catholic Conference for Interracial Justice in Chicago, July 27, 1963, Rabbi Balfour Brickner, director of the Commission on Interfaith Activities of the Union of American Hebrew Congregations, generously conceded "that the non-synagogued groups have been involved in civil rights issues prior to the awakening of Jewry's religious groups."

Now to Dr. Caplovitz' paper, which I had the opportunity to study in the advance copy he provided: I should say that in it we have much illuminating background material and an excellent frame of reference, but we need additional research on the specifically Jewish elements in the consumer relations he depicts. I hope he will, through the bureau of social research with which he is connected at the University of Chicago, help develop this research. Perhaps this Conference itself will stimulate research into the facts of Negro-Jewish consumer relations so that we can fortify impressions that are sound and repudiate impressions that are unsound or exaggerated.

Dr. Caplovitz shows that exploitative market relations breed contempt by the merchant for the customer, sometimes coupled with formal, contrived politeness to get his trade. This contempt, this attitude of superiority toward the Negro, the Puerto Rican or similar customer, will generally be transferred to that minority group as a whole, and Jewish leadership has a responsibility to cope with these attitudes of white superiority which are fed in this kind of market relationship. Furthermore, contempt provokes resentment, hostility and hatred on the part of the super-exploited customer when he accidentally or in some other way gradually learns that he is overcharged and otherwise victimized. And where the offending merchant is a Jew, the offended customer would have to be socially sophisticated indeed to distinguish between the merchant as a member of an exploitative economic class and the merchant's Jewishness as an irrelevant ethnic fact. Antisemitic propaganda feeds on the confusion of these two categories. The resulting antisemitism is nasty but futile, for the customer will not solve his problem simply by "blaming the Jews."

Dr. Caplovitz also pointed out that "as the Negro community becomes more self-conscious of its rights" and steps up its pace of activities, the problems of Negro-Jewish relations in this ghettoized marketing context will become sharper. The Jewish leadership is aware of this and has been discussing it. There is not only concern but a growing sense of responsibility.

This morning, I may say, Dean Horace Mann Bond finally shocked all of us into a greater awareness of the responsibility that, he insisted, all white people share for what he called "the brutalization, degradation and deculturation" of the Negro people. Thus I, and each of us, bear some responsibility for a Governor Wallace and for the still unpunished murderers of the four Negro girls in the Birmingham Sunday School. Thus I, and each of us, bear some responsibility that Mr. Cohen, head of Plumbers Union Local 2, has in effect been excluding Negroes and Puerto Ricans from his local. To deny this responsibility, is simply to seem evasive—and the Negro will not accept this evasion.

What can we do about the responsibility which Dr. Bond pointed out we Jews bear as white people? First, I think we have much to learn from the remark by Mr. Bayard Rustin at the Luncheon Session, that what the Negro people need from us is not so much *sympathy* (compassion or commiseration) as *empathy*, an appreciative understanding of their living conditions and situation. Thus, with reference to the incident, often mentioned today, of the attack by Negro children on the pupils of the Brownsville Yeshiva, I can say that I have no *sympathy* with the Negro children, a product of the totally inadequate education we New Yorkers have provided for them, who attacked the Yeshiva boys—but I can have *empathy* with them, understanding that if I were so desperate, frustrated and ignorant, I might have been among that group, striking out blindly and savagely and in utter futility. For the Yeshiva boys, I may add, I have both empathy and sympathy, and I even defend their right to be "queer and strange," as one of our sociologists called them this morning, in a democracy which should recognize the right to be "queer and strange" without being branded as "deviant" in sociological jargon.

Secondly, I believe I can rid myself of continuing responsibility only by continuing activity against all kinds of "brutalization, degradation and de-culturation" of the Negro people. I can rid myself of responsibility for Mr. Cohen of the Plumbers Union only by diassociating myself from his policy, by conspicuously advancing an opposite program and acting on it vigorously.

Now it is a fact that Negroes expect more of Jews than they do of non-Jewish liberals or of non-Jews in general. For example, *Fortune* magazine in February, 1960, quoted two Negro public figures on this subject. One of them, Joseph Overton, then a local leader of the National Association for the Advancement of Colored People, in commenting on tensions between Negroes and Jews in Harlem at the time as a result of the fact that white liquor dealers in Harlem were "closed to Negro salesmen," said: "Most of the white businessmen in Harlem are Jewish, and I thought that they should understand from the long business relationship the nature of this problem. I expressed amazement (before the city's Commission on Intergroup Relations) that a people who had suffered so much from discrimination should itself discriminate." More explicit even than that was James Baldwin's remark that "an understanding is expected of the Jew such as none but the most naive and visionary Negro has ever expected of the American Gentile. . . . " And this morning Dr. Bond has also expressed his particular disappointment about the position of southern Jews on the issue of segregation.

What should our reaction be to this fact that Negroes expect more of Jews than they do of others? First, we should note that this expectation does not arise from any mystical concept of the superiority of the Jews as a "chosen people." This expectation arises from the Negroes' perception, and in part from our telling them, that we have had an experience of centuries of persecution, including a very recent experience with genocide. The Negroes presume that this experience has taught us something. Is our answer to be, "No, we have learned nothing from our history of persecution in antiquity or in the recent past. We are just as insensitive as any and every other white American"?

Some might come to such a conclusion on the ground that this is a "democratic" approach, that "equality" for Jews should include the assumption of equality in insensitivity to the Negroes' repressed position. But this approach does not make sense, first of all because the Jewish people *have* learned something from their historic and contemporary experience with antisemitic hostility of all kinds, from genocide to discrimination and prejudice. By and large the American Jewish population *has* developed a greater sensitivity to the Negro situation, and Jewish leadership, it seems to me, is responsible for harnessing this sensitivity and bringing it into action.

As I began to indicate, Jewish leadership has been discussing these problems. At the National Community Relations Advisory Council's annual meeting, June 27-30, 1963, many workshops were conducted on the role of Jewish community relations "in meeting the civil rights dilemma." There was acute awareness of the "persistent gap between the positions taken by major agencies of the Jewish community and the positions held by members of the Jewish community at large" (this and the following quotations are from Stanley Winkelman's "Consolidated Report" of these workshops). The workshops advised the constituent groups of the NCRAC, which include the majority of the Jewish population in our country, to undertake an intensive educational program in all temples, centers, chapters, lodges and groups on this question of Jewish participation in the struggle for Negro equality. My own observation has been that still more education is needed, because the gap between general pronouncement and widespread Jewish participation on a local and neighborhood basis is still great.

The NCRAC conference, moreover, also began discussing what to do about these notorious Jewish landlords, employers and merchants who are in excessive exploitative relationships to Negro tenants, workers, customers and clients. On the one hand, the NCRAC reaffirmed "our traditional position that there is no Jewish communal responsibility for the behavior of individual Jews . . . " On the other hand, "the workshops heard many reports of interventions by Community Relations Councils—either through approaches by individual leaders or formally by the CRC itself—in efforts to persuade merchants, realtors and other businessmen to change their attitudes or practices." Overtly rejecting the "moralistic" approach as suitable only for "sermons, talks to synagogue groups and the like," the workshops found "it was the concensus that the CRC, in dealing with individual employer or businessman, should be practical, stressing the individual's self-interest in the light of the dynamics of the developing situation. . . . "

The ambivalence of first denying communal responsibility and then acting on the premise that there is such responsibility is noteworthy. The ambivalence is rooted in a complex and changing situation, and in a gap between liberal theory and public practice. Personally, I hate all forms of exploitation and am opposed to an exploitative society. At the same time, I believe in full equality for Jews (and all people) and in the exercise of their democratic rights. In a certain sense, therefore, in an exploitative society, Jews have "as much" right as non-Jews to be exploitative, and antisemites (like Coughlin) who concentrate their denunciation of exploitation only on the minor Jewish component in the general exploitation are misleading the victims of exploitation from a real understanding of their exploitation. But, as the NCRAC implicitly recognizes, the exercise by Jews of this "right to exploit in an exploitative society" may lead to special consequences harmful to the Jewish community and in the long run even to the individual Jewish exploiter. Hence the NCRAC's efforts to "change their attitudes and practices." In this connection, Dr. Caplovitz has shown us that the Negro dollar has less purchasing value than the white dollar because of residential segregation. This fact puts to the test another liberal catchword, "equal pay for equal work." The question is, equal where: in the pay envelope or on the merchant's counter? As Dr. Caplovitz indicates in the very title of his book, *The Poor Pay More*—and the Negro and Puerto Rican poor pay still more. Yet no trade union has even begun to pay attention to this crying imbalance, in which Negroes pay much more for inferior goods and services than do non-ghettoized whites. Now it may be impossible to change that situation until you abolish the Harlems of our cities and get integrated housing on a mass scale, but certainly an awareness of this matter is necessary to adequate programming.

Recent data suggest that, in pursuit of the line suggested by the NCRAC, the beginnings of a program are emerging. First, there was an announcement by the Manhattan Chapter of the Congress of Racial Equality (*New York Post*, May 24, 1964) that the Chapter had initiated a program to "equalize the distribution of Negro businessmen in the Harlem area" by pressing white Harlem merchants to take in Negroes as partners. The Chapters pointed out that on 125th Street, Harlem's central shopping center, "only two of more than 300 businesses are owned and controlled by Negroes." I may add that there are very many Jewish-owned businesses on that street, but exact figures are unavailable. Failure to admit Negroes to partnership, the Chapter indicated, might lead to an economic boycott of white merchants in Harlem.

The New York Times, June 18, 1964 reported a positive development in the same direction. As far back as October 1963, the American Jewish Congress and the Urban League of Greater New York had sponsored the Interracial Council for Business Opportunity (co-chairmen are Rodman Rockefeller and Harvey C. Russell, vice-president of the Pepsi-Cola Co.), to provide technical advice and loans for Negro businessmen in New York. With grants of $30,000 from the Rockefeller Brothers Fund and the New York Foundation, the Council late in 1964 had a staff of three which was working with some 180 clients, of whom about 25 per cent were Negro businessmen outside the Negro ghettos and about 40 per cent were Negroes trying to get into business. Several Negro businessmen have already been aided to get loans ranging from $1,500 to $15,000 they would not otherwise have obtained. Similar Interracial Councils are being set up in Newark and Los Angeles and it is planned to establish in all cities that have both Urban League and American Jewish Congress chapters. The Council found that only 18 per cent of Harlem retail businesses are Negro-owned and that in New York as a whole only 12 Negro-owned businesses employ more than 10 persons. Already 14 commercial banks have agreed to cooperate with the Council in handling loan applications, and assistance is being sought from the Federal Small Businessmen's Administration. The address of the Council is 15 E. 84th St., New York, the offices of the American Jewish Congress. This development also ties in with the chartering of the new

Freedom Bank in Harlem, the first local banking institution in the area in which Negro capital will be dominant, and in which Jewish capital and banking administrative ability are also being used.

On an entirely different scale and in a quite different form but with a quite similar aim is the action of a group of Jewish young men who, only a few days ago, on April 29, 1964, picketed the New York Board of Rabbis. Calling themselves The Zealots, the group is headed by David Gurin, a student of city planning and a Harvard graduate. The circular which was handed out by the pickets and which came as a press release to my editorial offices, begins with a quotation from Isaiah and goes on:

> We petition the rabbis of New York to seek out the slum owners in their congregations and to threaten them with denunciation from the pulpit and even *herem* or excommunication if they fail to repair and maintain their properties.
>
> Surely the New York Board of Rabbis must be as embarrassed and angered as we are with the overabundance of Jewish names among the city's worst slum landlords. These men may be "honorable" members of the synagogue, but they are guilty of criminal practices which bring anguish to the lives of thousands of slum dwellers. . . .
>
> The majority of buildings with 50 or more violations listed in the *New York Times,* January 24, 1963, have identifiably Jewish landlords. Most of 600 buildings whose tenants have complained to housing "clinics" and tenants councils on the Lower East Side have Jewish landlords. Tenants in 80 buildings on the Lower East Side resorted to the rent strike in their quest for decent shelter. The landlords in 74 of these buidlings are Jewish. This means that over 1,500 Lower East Side families feel that the conditions under which they are forced to live are about as bad as no shelter at all—for they are willing to risk eviction. Who is their enemy? The landlord. Although some of the rent strikers and their leaders are Jewish, the landlord is also clearly Jewish. . . .
>
> As Jewish youth, we petition the rabbis of New York to uphold our historic standards of social justice, standards that demand more, not less, than those promulgated by the city. There are landlords who will claim they want to get rid of their properties, that rent control limits their profits. We urge the establishment of a non-profit Jewish Foundation to rehabilitate tenements at low cost.
>
> We have submitted to the rabbis a list of 250 Jewish landloards who own 500 slum buildings in Manhattan. The House of Israel must be cleansed of those who exploit the poor.

These young Jews took to the streets with their picketing and their circular. Are their proposals merely visionary? There is still another area in which Jewish organizations are showing concern and developing inner discussions on program. This is the "touchy" subject of what has been improperly called "preferential treatment" for Negroes to help them overcome the handicaps that have been thrust upon them in the century since the Emancipation Proclamation. On October 23, 1963, the City Commission on Human Rights of New York became the first government agency on any level that took a clear position in favor of such a special approach to the Negro people. The Chairman of the Commission, the Hon. Stanley H. Lowell, is also a vice-president of the American Jewish Congress (which recently distributed for chapter discussion pro and con position papers on the issue—papers weighted, it seemed to me, con).

The Commission statement took issue with the traditional liberal concept of a "color-blind society, by which we have meant that the 'color' of an individual should not deprive him in any way of his fair share of the essentials of our life—schooling, housing and employment." In contrast, the Commission declared: "For a hundred years the deliberate 'color-consciousness' of a prejudiced and unconcerned white majority has placed the Negro at a competitive disadvantage that cannot be eliminated by old method and old means." Declaring that "society must work affirmatively for integration rather than negatively for desegregation," the Commission called for special measures in education, housing and employment "to deal with the historic and existing exclusion pattern of our society." Rejecting both a "quota system" and "tokenism," the Commission called for a "conscious effort to find employment for qualified Negroes, wherever they have been barred in the past" and for special training to help Negroes qualify. In an address November 17, 1963 at a breakfast of the Public Employees Lodges of the Anti-Defamation League of B'nai B'rith, Mr. Lowell elaborated and restated the Commission policy. (Although the ADL and B'nai B'rith did not publish this address, it was issued by the City Commission itself and reprinted by *Jewish Currents,* Sept., 1964.) The issue, as I see it, is one of abolishing the privileges that white people have arrogated to themselves in the century since Emancipation. One cannot equalize the situation of the Negro people and make "equal opportunity" a meaningful phrase instead of a cynical slogan unless one works to abolish these white privileges. I do not underestimate the complexities or the difficulties, but such an approach is indispensable for the struggle for Negro equality.

It seems to me that what we who are committed to the civil rights struggle need to do is to work for the abolition of all white privileges that white people have assumed at the expense of the Negro people and some other groups like the Puerto Ricans on the mainland. The abolition of white privilege is a continuation of the old abolitionist struggle against slavery. Plumbers who have jobs because Negroes have not been taken into the union have arrogated to themselves privileges that they have no legal or moral right to enjoy. Some trade unionists somewhere have to say that, even if the Jewish Labor Committee does not.

Is it going to be difficult to persuade people of this approach? Very difficult. *Newsweek,* in its poll, published October 21, 1963, on what white people think of Negroes, found that opposition to what is called "preferential treatment" was higher than to any other aspect of the civil rights struggle.

Thus there are more white people, according to this poll, opposed to equalization or "preferential treatment" for Negroes in jobs and other opportunities than there are opposed to intermarriage between Negro and white! The old bugaboo about intermarriage has been replaced by the new bugaboo about "preferential treatment." But somewhere in the labor movement, the radical movement and in the ranks of the Jewish people, the leadership will have to begin taking a stand for the abolition of white privilege.

A Jewish trade union leader, Arthur Osman, executive vice-president of the Retail, Wholesale and Department Store Union, AFL-CIO, finally came forward with such a proposal in the *RWDSU Record*, Aug. 23, 1964, in an article entitled, " 'Reparations' Can End Racial Strife." Mr. Osman wrote:

> As a result of the crimes committed against them, most Negroes are desperately poor, uneducated and unable to compete with those who progressed at their expense and are equipped with advantages the Negro never had. What Negroes want is for America to repair the damage it has done to them. This can be done not by merely giving the Negroes "rights" but by giving them reparations, or privileges, if you will. They are entitled to and need to be awarded damages of sufficient scope to enable them to quickly rise to equal footing with the rest of the nation.
>
> The most practical start towards a solution would be to recognize the right of every Negro to a full education and to pay to every Negro who is willing to go to school (academic or vocational) an adequate subsistence wage. Secondly, every Negro family with school age children should receive financial subsidies sufficient to enable the mother to stay at home and take proper care of them. These two steps, which should not be charity but acts of elementary justice, can result in taking hundreds of thousands out of the labor market, off the streets, and directing them into efforts to become better and more valuable human beings, better equipped to make a contribution to the well-being of the nation.

Similarly a Negro leader, Whitney M. Young, Jr., executive director of the National Urban League, has spelled out a vast program for a special effort in employment, education, housing, health and welfare for the Negro people in *To Be Equal,* published by McGraw-Hill.

I have one more point—and I wish Mr. Robinson had been able to stay to hear it. I believe there is need for a program and activity against antisemitism on the part of Negro leadership, including Negro labor leadership. I know that A. Philip Randolph, head of the American Negro Labor Council, has from time to time spoken up against antisemitism. But more systematic education against antisemitism among Negro people is necessary for the success of the Negro people's movement for equality. Just as we Jews have to combat attitudes of white supremacy among Jews in the interest of the Jewish people, in the interest of our democracy and the advance of social progress in our country, so it seems to me that even angry Negro leaders (and there is no Negro leader who is not justifiably angry) need to help the Negro people understand that antisemitism is a blind alley, *a trap for the Negro people.* No people has ever solved its real problems by antisemitism, for antisemitism is a diversion from the problem. And the Negro people cannot afford to be diverted from the main problem of white supremacy and white privileges into antisemitic channels.

Mr. Robinson has recognized that "the Jewish community has been most progressive, most liberal" in the struggle for Negro equality. Not only has it been; it seems to me it still is. But that is not enough. The pace of the Negro people is accelerating, is stepping up continually. We who have been among the best allies of the Negro people in this struggle face one vital question: can we step up our pace in the alliance so that we do not become a *brake* on the alliance? As the struggle goes into more intense forms, the Negro people will brook no brakes and will turn against allies, no matter what their services or past record, who seem to retard the struggle. Our efforts therefore, it seems to me, have to be concentrated on interpreting to the Jewish people the justness of the goals of the Negro movement for equality, the understandable impatience of the Negro people 101 years after Emancipation, and the necessity for ever more extensive and intensive efforts to work with them to expand American democracy by achieving Negro equality.

SUMMATION

By SIGMUND DIAMOND

The task to which I have been assigned—that of commenting on the papers that have been delivered here and of finding some common theme or principle among them—reminds me in a somewhat perverse way of Heywood Broun's classic explanation of how he happened to become a socialist. It was all the fault, he said, of Thomas Nixon Carver, his professor of economics at Harvard University. Now since Professor Carver was widely known to be extremely conservative, Broun's explanation was a bit puzzling—and he was required to discuss the matter more fully. During the spring semester each year Carver gave a course on Comparative Economic Systems, and it was his practice during the first part of the course to invite socialists, communists, anarchists, syndicalists, and the like to present their side of the case, which he would then refute personally during the second part of the course. But by that time, as Broun recalled, spring had arrived, and with it the opening of the baseball season, and he cut class frequently to watch the Boston Red Sox play. The result was that he never heard the refutation, and all he remembered was the explosion of socialism. In a sense, then, Broun's clarity—or single-mindedness—arose from having heard too few signals. My confusion arises from having heard too many.

Much has been said here about what still remains to be learned in the field of race relations, but it is evident from what we have heard that a great deal has already been discovered. We know already, for example, a great deal about the psychological correlates of antisemitism and of anti-Negro prejudice; the literature on what has been called the authoritarian personality is enormous. Similarly, we know a great deal about the specific historical conditions under which racist ideologies develop.

We know that the general relationship between Jews and Negroes is materially influenced by the fact that there is so wide a discrepancy between the status in which they now normally encounter each other. The relationship between Jew and Negro is characteristically that of landlord and tenant, housewife and servant, employer and employee, merchant and customer, professional and client; and social and economic barriers reinforce racial differences. We know that levels of aspiration are related to actual performance and correlate with social class, and we know—within certain limits—what has to be done to raise levels of aspiration. We know, too, the enormous danger we create when, having motivated people to seek self-improvement, we systematically frustrate them by denying them the possibility of achieving what we have said they should aspire to achieve. And we know, finally, that in this effort some ethic must be found to mobilize the energies of people so that their behavior will be directed into channels we would all agree are desirable.

But to say even this much is really to play Hamlet without the Prince. Another theme, even if stated in somewhat muted fashion, has run through a number of these papers, and where it has been ignored the omission has, at least to me, been glaring. Clearly we are concerned not only with *understanding* a situation—the relations between Jews and Negroes in contemporary America—but also with *changing* it.

And having said that, we are immediately involved in another problem— the planning of peaceful social change—where, admittedly, we know far less and where, if we are to be honest, we must agree that there is far less agreement about goals. I have been told that my task is to reconcile the differences in point-of-view that have been stated in these papers, but even if I were far more perspicacious than I am I could not do so. I cannot do so because these differences are fundamentally related to totally different conceptions of what a good society would be and what is required to achieve that good society. I know of no scientific principle which can determine our goals for us or which can tell us what an appropriate rate of progress toward those goals would be. It is for this reason, of course, that the same developments in race relations which can be cited approvingly by one of our speakers can be dismissed as highly unsatisfactory by another. It may be a truism—but even truisms may be worth stating—that the accomplishment of social change requires the clarification of goals and the mobilization of people.

Hopefully, this annual meeting of the Conference on Jewish Social Studies has contributed to the clarification of goals. The rest is up to each of us.

SELECTED BIBLIOGRAPHY

COMPILED BY ABRAHAM G. DUKER

ABBREVIATIONS: AJ–*American Judaism;* AJS–*American Journal of Sociology;* CB–*Congress Bi-Weekly;* CCARJ–*CCAR Journal;* CJ–*Conservative Judaism;* CJF–*Chicago Jewish Forum;* Com–*Commentary;* CW–*Congress Weekly;* JC–*Jewish Currents;* JD–*The Jewish Digest;* JF–*Jewish Frontier;* JO–*Jewish Observer;* JJCS–*Journal of Jewish Communal Service;* JS–*Jewish Spectator;* JSWF–*Jewish Social Work Forum;* Jud–*Judaism;* Mid–*Midstream;* NC–*New Currents;* NJM–*National Jewish Monthly;* NJPO–*National Jewish Post and Opinion;* Rec–*The Reconstructionist;* RE–*Religious Education*

The serious student will find additional material in the publications of the American Jewish Committee (especially *The Committee Reporter*), the American Jewish Congress, the Anti-Defamation League of B'nai B'rith (especially *The ADL Bulletin*), Council of Jewish Federations and Welfare Funds, The Jewish Labor Committee, National Jewish Welfare Board (*The JWB Circle*), the National Community Relations Advisory Council, and local community relations councils. Additional items will be found in the compiler's article in this book, particularly notes 3, 5, 10 and 17. The *National Jewish Post and Opinion* also devotes much space to this question.

Regrettably, items from the Yiddish dailies could not be included. In particular, the columns by A. Menes in *The Forward* as well as those by Jacob Glatstein and B. Z. Goldberg in *The Day-Morning Journal* deserve the attention of the serious reader. The *Yiddisher Kemfer* (particularly M. Kalikstein's articles) is also of value.

Special thanks are due to Harry Alderman, librarian of the Blaustein Library of The American Jewish Committee, for his very helpful cooperation.

Alpert, Carl, "A Jewish Problem in the South," Rec, 12, March 22, 1946, 10-14.
American Jewish Committee, Blaustein Library, *Negro-Jewish Relations; A Selective Bibliography,* New York, April 30, 1963 (mimeo.), Compiled by Iva Cohen.
American Jewish Committee, New York Chapter, Kleinfeld, M. J. and Levinson, Louise, eds., *Negro Press Digest,* published irregularly (mimeo.).
American Jewish Congress, Metropolitan Council, *A Program for Integrating New York City's Schools,* New York, 1964 (processed).
Aronowitz, Alfred G., "The Maccabees Ride Again," *Saturday Evening Post,* June 27-July 4, 1964, 32, 34-36.
Aronson, Arnold, "Sectarianism in the American Society Today; Impact on Jewish Communal Services," JJCS, 42, Winter 1965, 139-51.
Baldwin, James, "The Harlem Ghetto: Winter 1948. The Vicious Circle of Frustration and Prejudice," Com, 5 Feb. 1948, 165-70.
Band, Jordan C., *The Human Rights Revolution. Role and Relation of Federation,* New York, Council of Jewish Federations and Welfare Funds, 1964, 8 pp. (proc.).

"The Birmingham Resolution," [a Discussion by Mordecai Kaplan, Everett Gendler, et al.], Proceedings of the Rabbinical Assembly of America, 27, 1963, 239-45.

Bloom, Jack, see "Jews and the Racial Crisis."

Braiterman, Marvin, see "The Civil Rights Front."

Brickner, Balfour, "New Jewish Initiative in the Field; A Report Presented before the National Catholic Conference for Interracial Justice," July 27, 1963, New York, Union of American Hebrew Congregations, 1963, 7 pp. (proc.).

Brody, Eugene B. and Derbyshire, Robert L., "Prejudice in American Negro College Students," *Archives of General Psychiatry,* 9, Dec. 1963, pp. 619-28.

"Changing Race Relations and Jewish Communal Service: A Symposium," JJCS, 41, Summer 1965, pp. 323-64; articles by Arthur Hertzberg, Albert D. Chernin.

Chernin, Albert D., *Notes for Statement on Jewish Communal Services and Civil Rights,* National Conference of Jewish Communal Services, Committee on Public Issues (draft), Jan. 21, 1964, 10 pp. (proc.).

————, see also "Changing Race Relations."

Chiel, Samuel, see "Jews and the Racial Crisis."

"The Civil Rights Front," Mid, 10, 3, Sept. 1964, 15-35; articles by Albert Vorspan, Ted Poston, Marvin Braiterman.

Clark, Dennis, "Urban Negro and Urban Jew," *The Crisis,* 65, May 1958, 275-80.

Clark, Kenneth B., "Candor about Negro-Jewish Relations," Com, 1, Feb. 1946, 8-14.

————, "The New Negro Faces the Jewish People," JC, 14, 8(157), Sept. 1960, 7-10.

Cohen, Iva, see American Jewish Committee.

Cohen, Jacob X., "Fighting Together for Equality," CW, 11, Nov. 3, 1944, 9-12.

————, "The Negro and Anti-Semitism," CW, 11, Dec. 22, 1944, 5-8.

Cohen, Seymour J., *The Negro-Jewish Dialogue,* New York, Synagague Council of America, 1963, reprinted in part from JS and Gesher (Nov. 1962).

Collins, Charles W., see Worthy, William.

Crystal, Moshe, "The Negro Riots and the Struggle for Civil Rights," *Zukunft,* 69, Sept. 1964, 298-99; 326-27.

Ellis, Eddie, "Semitism in the Black Ghetto," *Liberator,* 6, 1, Jan. 1966, 6-7; 2, Feb. 1966, 14-15.

Fenster, Myron M., "The Princeton Plan Comes to Jackson Heights," Mid, 10, 1, March 1964, 76-83.

————, "The Princeton Plan—One Year Later," Mid, 11, 2, June 1965, 68-73.

Fiedler, Leslie A., "Negro and Jew—Encounter in America," Mid, 2, 3, Summer 1956, 5-17; reprinted in *The Midstream Reader,* Shlomo Katz, ed., New York, Yoseloff, 1960, 27-44.

Fishman, Joshua, "Southern City," Mid, 7, 3, Summer 1961, 39-56.

Flascher, Charles W., see Worthy, William.

Gaba, Morton J., "Segregation and a Southern Jewish Community," JF, 21, Oct. 1954, 12-15.

Gendler, Everett, see "The Birmingham Resolution."

Gibel, Inge Lederer, "The Negro-Jewish Scene: A Personal View," Jud, 14, Winter 1965, 12-21.

Glazer, Nathan, "City Problems and Jewish Responsibilities," Com, 33, Jan. 1962, 24-30.

————, "Effects of Emerging Urban-Suburban and Anti-Segregation Developments on Jewish Communal Service," JJCS, 41, Fall 1964, 60-66.

————, "Negroes and Jews: The New Challenge to Pluralism," Com, 38, Dec. 1964, 29-34.

————, "Jews and Poverty," Mid, 12, 1, Jan. 1966, 30-36.

Glazer, Nathan, and Moynihan, Daniel P., *Beyond the Melting Pot: The Negroes, Puerto Ricans, Jews, Italians, and Irish of New York City,* Cambridge, Mass., M.I.T. Press and Harvard University Press, 1963.

Glicksberg, Charles I., "The Negro and the Jew," CJF, 5, Summer 1947, 229-33.

Golden, Harry, "Negro Intellectuals and White Liberals," CB, 32, Nov. 15, 1965, 10-11.

————, "Unease in Dixie," Mid, 2, 4, Autumn 1956, pp. 38-51.

Goodman, Arnold M., "The Equity of Redemption," Rec, 3, April 2, 1965, pp. 7-13.

Gordis, Robert, *Race and the Religious Tradition,* New York, Anti-Defamation League of B'nai B'rith, 1963, 23 pp. Reprint of a chapter in *The Root and the Branch,* Chicago, University of Chicago Press, 1962.

Gordon, Albert I., "Negro-Jewish Marriages: Three Interviews," Jud, 13, Spring 1964, 164-84; also printed in his *Intermarriage,* Boston, Beacon Press, 1964, pp. 263-95.

Gumbiner, Joseph H., "Purim in Alabama," Rec, 31, May 28, 1965, 24-31.

Halpern, Ben, "The Destinies of Jew and Negro," JF, 14, Nov. 1947, 19-23.

————, *see also* Teller, Judd L.

Harap, Louis, "Anti-Negroism among Jews," *The Negro Quarterly,* 1, Summer 1942, 105-111.

Harris, Joseph, "Block Busting and the Role of the East New York YM & YWHA," JSWF, 1, 2, Spring 1964, 46-53.

Heller, Celia Stopnicka and Pinkney, Alphonso, "The Attitude of Negroes toward Jews," *Social Forces,* 43, March 1965, 364-69.

Hero, Alfred C., "Southern Jews, Race Relations and Foreign Policy," *Jewish Social Studies,* 27, Oct. 1965, pp. 213-35.

Hertz, Richard C., "Rising Tide of Negro-Jewish Tensions," *Ebony,* 20, Dec. 1964, 117-25.

Hertzberg, Arthur, *see* "Changing Race Relations."

Israel, Edward L., "Jew Hatred Among Negroes," *The Crisis,* 43, Feb. 1936, 39, 50.

"Jews and the Civil Rights Movement" (editorial), Rec, 31, Oct. 1, 1965, 3-4.

"Jews and the Racial Crisis," *Conservative Judaism,* 19, Summer 1965, 1-27; articles by Charles Silberman, Paul Lauter, Jack Bloom, Samuel Chiel.

Kahn, William, "Confrontation in a Jewish Center between a Resolution on Equal Opportunities and Practical Reality," JJCS, 42, Winter 1965, 163-70.

Kaplan, Mordecai M., *see* "The Birmingham Resolution."

Karpatkin, Marvin M., "A Journey to New Orleans," CJF, 23, Winter 1964-1965, 124-30.

Laufer, Leo, "Anti-Semitism Among Negroes," Rec, 14, Oct. 1948, 10-17.

Lauter, Evelyn, "Some 'Mixed Marrieds' Speak for Themselves," NJM, 79, 4, Dec. 1964, 14-15.

Lauter, Paul, *see* "Jews and the Racial Crisis."

Levenson, Paul H., "The Image of the Jew in the Negro Community," JC, 16, 8(179), Sept. 1962, 7-12.

Liberson, David, "The Negro Problem in America, Now and Before (Historical Comparison and Conclusions)," *Zukunft,* 69, Oct. 1964, 379-90.

Lurie, Walter A., *The Best Lack All Conviction. Some Reflections on the Role of Jewish Communal Agencies in the Crisis of our Times,* Philadelphia, Association of Jewish Agency Executives of Philadelphia, Dec. 5, 1963, 7 pp. (proc.).

MacMillan, Lewis K., "The Negro Forty-Ninth State in the Light of the Jewish National Home," *Journal of Negro Education,* 9, 1940, 144-53.

Malev, William S., "The Jew of the South in the Conflict on Segregation," CJ, 13, Fall 1958, 35-46.

Mantinband, Charles, "Integration and the Southern Jew," CW, 25, 11, June 16, 1958, 9-11.

————, *see also,* Nussbaum, Perry E.; "Seminar on Civil Rights."

Maslow, Will, "Negro-Jewish Relations," in Westin, Alan M., Ed., *Freedom Now! The Civil Rights Struggle in America,* New York, Basic Books, 1964, pp. 297-301.

————, "Negro-Jewish Relations in the North," *Proceedings of the Association of Jewish Community Relations Workers' Conference,* Arden House, 1960, 4 pp. (mimeo.).

McLaurin, Benjamin F., *see,* Teller, Judd L.

Miller, Carl L., *see* "Seminar on Civil Rights."

Miller, Charles, "The Impact of the Integration Struggle Upon Jewish Communal Services," JJCS, 41, Fall 1964, 67-74.

Millman, Herbert, "The Jewish Community Center and Civil Rights," The JWB Circle, 19, 1, Jan. 1964, 1-2, 6.

Morsell, John A., "Jewish Community Agencies and Negro-Jewish Relations," *Proceedings of the Association of Jewish Community Relations Workers' Conference,* Arden House, 1960, [New York] 10 pp. (mimeo.).

Moss, James A., "The American Jew and the Negro Civil Rights Struggle," CJF, 23, Fall 1965, pp. 15-18.

Muravchik, Emanuel, "Troubled Allies," *Jewish Life,* 30, 3 March-April 1963, 9-16.

"Negroes and Jews in America" [a youth symposium], *Our Age,* 7, 9, Feb. 13, 1966, pp. 1-4.

Nussbaum, Perry E.; Mantinband, Charles; Rothschild, Jacob M., "The Southern Rabbi Faces the Problem of Desegregation," CCARJ, 14, June 1956, 1-16.

Nussbaum, Perry E., "And Then There Was One—In the Capital City of Mississippi," CCARJ, 11, 3, Oct. 1963, pp. 15-19.

Offord, Carl, "Slave Markets in the Bronx," *The Nation,* 150, June 29, 1940, 780-81.

Palnick, Elijah E., "Southern Jewry and Civil Rights," CCARJ, 22, .2, June 1965, 62-65.

Podhoretz, Norman, "My Negro Problem—And Ours," Com, 35, Feb. 1963, 93-101; *see also* "Letters," *ibid.,* 35, 6, June 1963, 525-31; and Polier, Justine Wise and Shad, "Fear Turned to Hatred," CB, 30, Feb. 18, 1963, 5-7.

Polier, Justine Wise and Shad, *see* Podhoretz, Norman.

Polier, Shad, "The Jew and the Racial Crisis," CB, 21, Sept. 14, 1964, 5-8.

Poston, Ted, *see* "Civil Rights Front."

Potok, Chaim, "Reflections on a Bronx Street," Rec, 30, Oct. 30, 1964, 13-20.

Powell, Adam Clayton, Jr., "What Negroes Think About Jews," NC, 1, 6, Sept. 1943, 16.

"Racism Is Racism," (*editorial*) CB, 33, Feb. 21, 1966, 3-4.

Reddick, L. F. "Anti-Semitism Among Negroes," *The Negro Quarterly,* 1, Summer 1942, 112-122.

Richardson, Ben, "This Is Our Common Destiny. The Case for Negro and Jewish Unity," a series of articles in *The People's World,* New York, 1943, 8 pp.

Rothschild, Jacob M., "The Atlanta Story," AJ, 12, 1, Fall 1962, 8-9, 51-52.

———, "One Man's Meat . . . A Personal Experience," CCARJ, 13, 2, June 1965, 57-61.

———, *see also* Nussbaum, Perry E.

Rubenstein, Dan, "Attempts in the Practice of Integration in a Jewish Agency," JSWF, 2, 1, Winter 1964-65, 30-41.

Rubenstein, Richard L., "The Rabbi and Social Conflict," RE, 59, 1, Jan.-Feb. 1964, 100-06.

Schappes, Morris U., *see* Worthy, William.

Schick, Marvin, "The Orthodox Jew and the Negro Revolution," JO, 2, 3, Dec. 1964, 15-17.

"Seminar on Civil Rights," *Central Conference of American Rabbis Year Book,* 74, 1964, 235-53; contains papers by Carl L. Miller, Charles Mantinband, discussion.

Shapiro, Manheim S., "The Negro Revolution—and Jews," *Council Woman,* 26, April 1964, 7-10.

Sheppard, Harold L., "The Negro Merchant, A Study of Negro Anti-Semitism," AJS, 53, 2, Sept. 1947, 96-99.

Sherman, C. Bezalel, "In the American Jewish Community," JF, 31, 6, July 1964, 16-18.

Shulweis, Harold M., "The Voice of Esau," Rec, 31, Dec. 10, 1965, 7-14.

Silberman, Charles E., *see* Teller, Judd L.

Simpson, Richard L., "Negro-Jewish Prejudice: Authoritarianism and Some Social Variables as Correlates," *Social Problems,* 7, Fall 1959, 138-46.

Sobel, B. Z. and May, L., "Negroes and Jews: Minority Groups in Conflict," Jud, 15, Winter 1966, 3-22.

Stemons, James Sam, *As Victim to Victim. An American Negro Laments with Jews,* New York, Fortuny's, 1941.

Suritz, A. R., "A Southerner Looks at Jews in the South," NJM, 72, 9, June 1958, 4-5.

Syrkin, Marie, "Can Minorities Oppose 'de Facto' Segregation?" JF, 31, 8, Sept. 1964, 6-12; Discussion, Nov. 1964, 3-11.

———, "Anti-Semitic Drive in Harlem," CW, 8, Oct. 31, 1941, 6-8.

Tartakower, Aryeh, "Problem of Negro Antisemitism," *Hadoar,* 44, Oct. 16, 1964, 751-53.

Teller, Judd L., "Negro and Jew," JF, 30, Sept. 1963, pp. 9-13.

Teller, Judd L., and Guttman, Nahum, eds., *The Free World and the New Nations,* New York, A. S. Barnes, 1964, pp. 112-76 (contains articles by Charles E. Silberman, Ben Halpern, Benjamin F. McLaurin, and Judd L. Teller).

Vorspan, Albert, "The Negro Victory and the Jewish Failure," AJ, 13, 1, Fall 1963, 7, 50-53.

———, "Segregation in the North: A Challenge to the Jew," JF, March 1957, 11-13.

———, "Social Action Enters a New Era," AJ 13, 3, Spring 1964, 22-23.

Wax, James A., "The Attitude of the Jews in the South toward Integration," CCARJ, 26, June 1959, 14-20.

Wedlock, Lunabelle, *The Reaction of Negro Publications and Organizations to German Anti-Semitism, Howard University Studies in Social Sciences,* Washington, 1942, 3, 2.

Weinstein, Jacob, "Behind the Harlem Riots," JF, 2, May 1935, pp. 12-14.

———, "How One Congregation Faced the Problem of Integration," JF, 26, March 1959, 13-17.

Weiss-Rosmarin, Trude, "Negro Anti-Semitism," JS, 29, March 1964, 3-4.

Wilkins, Roy, "Jewish-Negro Relations: An Evaluation," AJ, 12, 3, Spring 1963, 4-5.

Wilson, James Q., *Negro Politics: The Search for Leadership,* New York, Free Press of Glencoe, 1960, 151-64.

Wittenstein, Charles F., "Jews, Justice and Liberalism," *New South* (Southern Regional Council), July-August 1965, 13-16.

Wolf, Arnold Jacob, "The Negro Revolution and Jewish Theology," Jud, 13, Fall 1964, 478-83.

Wolf, Eleanor Paperno; Loving, Alvin D.; Marsh, Donald C., *Negro-Jewish Relationships,* Detroit, Wayne University Press, 1944 (Wayne University Studies in Intergroup Conflicts in Detroit, no. 1).

Wolpe, Gerald I., "The Southern Jew and 'the Problem,' " Rec. 22, Dec. 14, 1956, 25-30.

Worthy, William; Collins, Charles W.; Flascher, Kurt; Schappes, Morris U., "New Developments and New Tensions in Negro-Jewish Relations," JC, 17, 5(187), May 1963, 4-25.

Zwerling, Mat, "Mississippi: Portrait of a Fighting People," JSWF, 2, 1, Winter 1964-65, 23-29.

Zuckerman, Nathan, *The Wine of Violence: An Anthology on Anti-Semitism,* New York, Association Press, 1947, 313-42.